ROCK EATER

ROCK EATER

MASON RODRIGUE

The .M249 Squad Automatic Weapon is an air cooled, belt fed, crew served(?), fully automatic, gas operated weapon chambered in 5.56 mm

— MASON F

Momma Bon Bon,
Thank you so much for
all you do for Book Club.
I hope you stay on the
team for the long haul.

Stay jacked
—MASON

Publisher: Dead Reckoning Collective
Book Cover Art & Design: Tyler James Carroll
Editor: Keith Walter Dow

Printed in the United States of America

ISBN-13: 978-1-7376686-7-1 (paperback)

DED. FOR MARINES

For Marines,
those still alive and those long dead,
Cammies woodland green and
Dress Blues blood striped red.
For Marines,
from recruits to Commandants,
And the barracks and battlefields
they'll all forever haunt.
For Marines,
from the freshest of boots
to the oldest of salts,
I love you all, my brothers,
In spite of all our faults.

PROLOGUE: DELAYED ENTRY

SECTION 1: BOOT

1.1. PARRIS ISLAND

1.2. BOOT DROP

1.3. SYRIA

1.4. POST DEPLOYMENT

SECTION 2: SECOND AWARD SENIOR

2.1. RESTRICTION

2.2. WORK UP

2.3. JAPAN

2.4. TERMINAL LEAVE

MATT'S EPILOGUE

I. Jaeger
II.Giants
III.Follow the Leader
IV.It Takes Something to Feel Alive

IT WAS "PEACETIME"

WAR WAS EVERYWHERE

FOREWORD ———————————

I was surprised that Mason asked me to write the foreword to his book. We met a year ago, and at the time, only on the internet, around when he decided to shed the veil of anonymity and let the world know he was the man behind an Instagram page. He had just left the Marine Corps, and it was not on the best of terms. Separation for most of us seems to happen in circumstances that are less than ideal for one reason or another. Some are better than others, but isn't that how life goes? I would imagine that's how it's always gone.

But really, I was surprised because of how different we are at face value. He was a machine gunner for the Marines who embodied the esprit de corps mentality. In comparison, I was a medic for the Army who resisted enlisting and was ready to get out when my contract was over. I'm married with four kids. He's single, and we're pretty sure he doesn't have any kids. But he's met mine, and not many people have.

Late last summer, Louisiana got hit by a hurricane (imagine that.) Fortunately, Mason got out in time. He let me know he was coming to the Dallas area for two to three weeks. One of the first nights he got into town, I invited him over to my house, and he insisted on making dinner for me, my wife, and four small kids. After leaving his apartment boarded up with plywood windows and driving nearly nine hours, he bought chicken, rice, Tony's cajun seasoning and sauce, pyrex dishes (even though I had some), and baked my family a meal. It was delicious.

After my kids went to bed, we made ourselves comfortable on my back patio. I made the mistake of saying that I wouldn't quit drinking until he did. He saw it as a challenge and came far more prepared than me, as I had been out of the binge drinking game (173rd Airborne Brigade) for nearly a decade.

At almost four in the morning, my wife texted me asking when I was coming to bed. She gave me out. And with a table full of empty Shiner Bocks, I submitted and stumbled my way into bed. I woke up the next morning with a throbbing headache, reminded that my mouth and ego tend to fail me.

That wasn't the first time I met Mason in person. A couple of months prior, we were in Montana together for a Patrol Base Abbate retreat, specifically for the book club. The week before the retreat, Mason was working at an oil refinery in the port of Louisiana. Most people from his hometown end up in those refineries.

He was making good money but felt like he had no purpose. It was a story I had heard dozens of times, most of which have predictable endings. Mason's story differs from those dozens of others in what he did just prior to coming to Montana. He realized there are more important things than money and stability, and with that thought, he quit his job to seek another opportunity. He was only supposed to be in Montana for a week, but he ended up staying there for three weeks acting as point man for the up-and-coming non-profit, mostly solving logistical problems, without any training. He heard a calling and answered it.

He later admitted that he knew I would be there and wanted to pitch his book and see what DRC was all about. With his kind of charisma and extroverted-militant mindset, we hit it off immediately. He reminded me of a machine gunner I deployed with to Afghanistan. There's a certain level of confidence required to be a legitimate brute. Mason had that kind of confidence. When shit hits the fan, I want the kind of man by my side that doesn't second guess himself and knows exactly what he's capable of.

Since starting this publishing company, I've read a lot of war poetry. Everyone experiences war and service differently, but you find it's difficult to find new ways of describing it. And when I met Mason, I wasn't exactly sure what he was going to offer. But when Mason read *Church* on my back patio, I knew this was a man more than what his exterior and experience portrayed. Mason is a thinker and a feeler, and a damn good poet. But at his core, he will always be a Marine, and he is okay with that. When I first spoke to him, he told me that rap and metal music influenced his poetry and that he wasn't trying to be anything he's not. You're going to get all of him from each of these poems without any smoke and mirrors or half stepping. It's a vulnerability most won't ever know.

This book may not end up in the halls of Harvard, but that's probably not where it belongs. However, poems in this book have been read to midshipmen at the Naval Academy so they can understand the type of Marine they will lead. You'll find this book lying on end tables in photos of young Marines time stamped in the archives of the United States Marine Corps. Whiskey-stained, this book will get passed around the barracks, and *that's* where it belongs. With those men who have tasted their own blood and made others taste theirs.

—TYLER JAMES CARROLL

PROLOGUE: DELAYED ENTRY

P.1. ADOLESCENCE —————

The towers fell a year before their marriage.
I still remember my father's rage,
Shouts of disparage.
"They should level the fucking Middle East into a
parking lot!"
I was just a little boy, my Father's Son,
I thought,
"Why not?"
A year later my mother left, it was such a shame.
I looked around wondering who to blame
for this marriage collapsed like the towers all the
same.
I drowned myself in a violent game,
Football and Alcohol to soothe pediatric child pain.
They said college is where I should go,
what I was doing there after football ended, I do not
know.
So I went talk to the recruiter at the OSO
to become a Marine officer with something to show
for that wasted time and useless degree
a bachelor of science just to lead the infantry.
New Orleans had other plans for me on Mardi Gras night-
at the jail after the DUI, the familiar sight:
My mother slowly began to cry.
I felt so low
I wanted to die.
Two years of probation working
at the refinery, I
said "fuck it" and enlisted infantry.
Maybe that uniform will give me a reason
to hold myself in higher esteem.
Maybe I can start my life over
as a U.S. Marine.
When I look back on all the wrong turns
I see that in essence
I was headed for Parris Island
since a troubled adolescence.
Searching for manhood through war
with the rest of the adolescents.

P.2. ORIGINAL SIN ————————————

I wanted
to know
war
and why
men fight.
Where they come from
how they bond,
and love,
And die.
I wanted to see
the guns
fire.
How men kill,
what violence they do.
Far away desolate lands that we go to.
Adventure turned sour and spoiled.
Forbidden fruits from
the Tree of Knowledge.
I left my Eden, said goodbye to my Eve
because I wanted to know.
"Knowledge is Power"
and
"Might makes Right."
When you're at war with yourself,
you make your whole life a fight.

P.3. (DON'T) FOLLOW ME ———————

Caffeine, nicotine
OD green enlisted Marine.
Not as lean, far more mean,
rather forget all he's seen.
All a blur, mostly obscene,
nightly cycle with the team.

Fist fights,
long nights
cigarettes
crippling debt
regret
can't sleep
cold sweat
nightmares
can't forget
love lost
counts costs
prices paid
choices made
dip spit
can't quit
can't cut
the bullshit.

Back hurts,
ears ring,
Lost track
of everything
Shooting pains,
rifle range
Tattoos,
Dress Blues,
Does it still sound
fun to you?

SECTION 1: BOOT

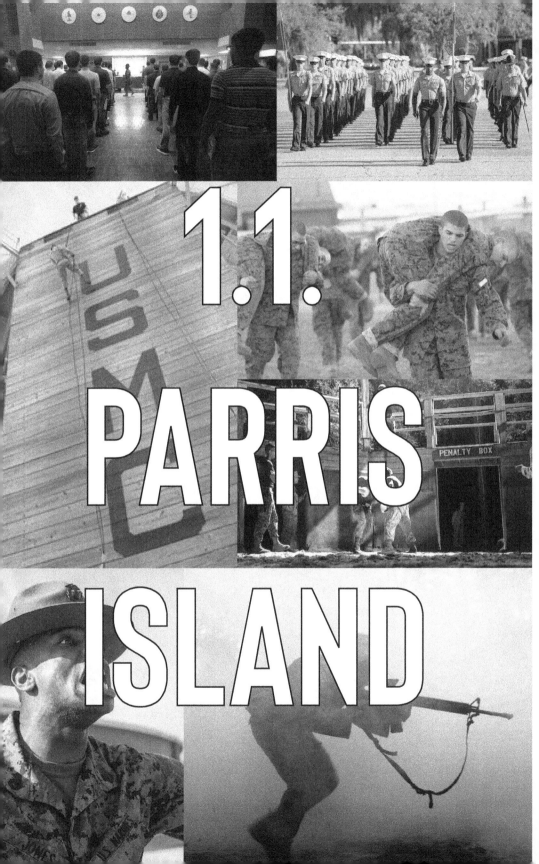

1.1.
PARRIS
ISLAND

1.1-1 THE BUS

It was a van,
then a hotel.
I had to turn the bathroom
into a sauna to cut weight;
Hell before my Hell.
Then it was a plane ride,
and a connecting flight.
Then finally
a big white bus
in the middle of the night,
picking up the next generation;
"First to Fight."
The kids were so excited
over where they were about to go.
I knew it was a timebomb,
waiting for us to arrive to explode.
The wheels on the bus
rolled round and round
we had arrived upon
cursed, hallowed ground.
Nervous chatter, boastful laughter.
Yellow footprints, silenced after.
They said "heads down!"
Not one fucking sound.
The DI's came onto the bus,
they got screams out of all of us.
Might as well be a hearse;
that big white USMC bus.
Oh, how they broke those kids
who wouldn't shut the fuck up.

1.1-2 MOMENT OF TRUTH

They played on our **Honor** to get us to snitch on
ourselves,
yet it didn't feel like **Courage** when I caved at the
Moment of Truth.
Unfortunately for me they needed every warm body they
could get
to see it through the full four year enlistment
of this insane **Commitment.**

I was worried I'd pop for weed on the piss test.
I told them up front and got it off my chest.
The meanest Master Sergeant grilled me,
looked like she wanted to kill me.
She was taller than me; burly and surly.
She thought I was a fuckup, surely.
She looked through my file; the dead-end degree,
now trying to enlist infantry.
She looked through my file and saw the probation
and the covered up DUI.

"What is this, some last ditch effort to not be a total
piece of shit?"
"No Ma'am" I lied.
I'm not sure why I didn't get fried.
But I do know that every last one of us
has something to hide.

1.1-3 ON LINE

We stood
rigid and on line.

Like little toy Marines
Rigid, at attention,
silence building tension,
Surprise on some kids' faces
as if their recruiter failed to mention
the DI's cruel intentions.
They burst through the door like rabid dogs,
barking and biting, they struck like lightning.
For some it was merely disorienting,
for others it was frightening.
All of this screaming, all of this yelling,
to condition us to be the kind of men
who can keep calm under shelling.
These men are sharks, weakness smelling.
When it ends, no telling.
Screaming and running,
up and down.
They threw everything we had left
all over the ground.
Then they disappeared

leaving us
rigid and on line.

1.1-4 LIGHTS

"LIGHTS! LIGHTS! LIGHTS!"

Like every night at 20:00
The squad bay, finally, a peaceful sight
of recruits in perfectly aligned racks
hoping to dream of home's delights.
The sound made me bolt upright-
Recruits screaming in panic and fright
a recruit rolled out of his rack and was seizing
tonight.
"ALL OF YOU AGAINST THE WALL RIGHT NOW!"
The DI had to handle this situation somehow.
I stood there in my skivvies facing the window
as the life
left the body
of the recruit
I barely got to know.
We were facing away,
as if not seeing meant we wouldn't know.
From three decks below
Red and blue lights
illuminated the squad bay.
We stood in silent attention, not a word we could say.
They took the kid's body away.
I don't even think he was twenty
and he died that day.
All he wanted was a spot in the fray,
and to wear blues with brothers
on the Marine Corps birthday.
Death is a price that many Marines pay,
But I still ask myself
"Why this way?"
"Why that night?"
We were ordered to go back to sleep, then
Like every morning at 04:00

"LIGHTS! LIGHTS! LIGHTS!"

1.1-5 THE RAIN ROOM —————————

Around 1700 every day
We stripped naked and
They herded us, all 85 of us,
Through a room with maybe 40 shower heads.
The water was cold.
I will never forget the way it stung,
The way it pulled the breath from our lungs.
In and out, the Kill Hat watched us, making us scream
and shout.
"TWO MINUTES, AYE SIR!"
This is how we showered every day, it still sounds
absurd.
They called it The Rain Room.

At night we turned it into The Pain Room.
Bald teenagers wrapped their hands in wash cloths,
The Firewatch kept guard,
One night the Kill Hat proudly watched.
The only rule of The Rain Room is if you watch, you must
fight.
We settled our scores and drew blood almost every night.
In Our Corps, Might makes Right.
In the morning we tell lies to cover for our black eyes.
"SIR! THIS RECRUIT FELL OUT HIS RACK!"
That recruit took a left hook he never saw coming.
That recruit was laid out on his back in a puddle.
Why did we do this to each other every other night?
Who wants to go to war with a man
who's afraid to fight?

1.1-6 CHOW TO CHOW

Two sheets and a blanket!
PT, Chow to Chow!
Drill Foot, Kill Foot!
Phase One, Two, Three,
"This Recruit" no longer me.
March and Drill and Drill and March,
Iron uniforms, use too much starch.
IT on the quarterdeck,
Scream until it hurts your neck.
Class and Knowledge,
these kids wish they'd gone to college.
Screaming cadence and doing burpees in the sand,
A rifle belongs nowhere but your hands.
Drill, Drill, Drill, Drill,
Kill, Kill, Kill, Kill.
Sprinting and Screaming,
kids shouting "AYE, SIR!"
in their racks
while they're dreaming,
We never know what
the DI's are scheming.
Scream out of your face
make your heart race
pick up the pace
get me the fuck out of this place.
MCMAP and fistfights,
write home at the end of the day.
Then it's lights out.
The only way out of here
is to get through it now.
Keep your sanity by making it
from chow to chow.

1.1-7 SCREAM

"**MARINE CORPS BIRTHDAY!**"
"SIR, MARINE CORPS BIRTHDAY IS
NOVEMBER 10, 1775, SIR!"
"**TWO MARINES, TWO MEDALS!**"
"SIR, TWO MARINES TWO MEDALS IS
DAN DALY AND SMEDLEY BUTLER, SIR!"
"**FIVE NAVY CROSSES!**"
"SIR, FIVE NAVY CROSSES IS
GENERAL CHESTY PULLER, SIR!"
"**JOHN BASILONE!**"
"SIR, JOHN BASILONE IS
GUADALCANAL AND IWO JIMA, SIR!"
"**HUE CITY!**"
"SIR, HUE CITY IS
HOUSE TO HOUSE
STREET TO STREET, SIR!"
"**FAILURE TO STOP!**"
"SIR, FAILURE TO STOP IS
TWO IN THE CHEST, ONE IN THE HEAD, SIR!"
"**FAILURE TO STOP!**"
"SIR, FAILURE TO STOP IS
TWO IN THE CHEST, ONE IN THE HEAD, SIR!"
"**FAILURE TO STOP!**"
"SIR, FAILURE TO STOP IS
TWO IN THE CHEST, ONE IN THE HEAD, SIR!"
"**TWO IN THE CHEST!**"
"ONE IN THE HEAD!"
"**TWO IN THE CHEST!**"
"ONE IN THE HEAD!"
"**TWO IN THE CHEST!**"
"ONE IN THE HEAD!"

1.1-8 THE RIFLE AND THE WEAPON ——

This is my rifle.
There are many like it, but this one is mine
until the end of recruit training.
It is not what I will be issued in the Fleet.
It is old, with the classic, thick, non adjustable
buttstock.
It has to be this way for us to learn to drill.
Even still, when I hold it, I imagine using it to kill.
The carry handle, the iron sights,
not the current technology we use to fight.
Still I think of aligning the front sight post
with the rear peep hole
for an enemy in my sight.
Thoughts of using my rifle in war
keep me warm in my rack at night.
The rifle is black,
the rifle is cold,
the rifle is useless,
it has no soul.
The rifle is one of many tools in the infantry;
How skillfully I use them depends
on how good a weapon
the Marine Corps makes me.
I am no longer Mason, I, or me,
I am This Recruit waiting to go condition one
against an enemy.

1.1-9 FIX BAYONETS

Sergeant Tom Lovell's canvas spoke to me
In a way Van Gogh speaks to people at art galleries.
The doughboy standing over a German soldier
reaching up in a plea for mercy
as the Marine plunges the bayonet
into his sprawled out enemy.
Belleau Wood.

The sheer violence of it,
surrounded by chaos
and hand to hand combat
Shook me
Made me question
If I could kill like that.

A month later
We fixed bayonets to our M16s
And sprinted through an obstacle course in the woods
To feel what it was like
To be those old Marines.
Run to the stack of tires,
Feel your heart race,
Plunge the bayonet into
Your enemies face.

Upstroke, Buttsroke
Slash and Thrust!
Against these tires
I unleashed
a growing bloodlust.
Upstroke, Buttstroke
Slash and Thrust!
Screaming war cries
to October skies.
Condition me
to fight or die.

The Crucible was only as bad as you believe it is.
If you're going infantry
it's only just a taste.
Three days came and went quicker than I thought they
would,
almost underwhelming.
We were so physically conditioned that all the running
and jumping and fighting
was just par the course.
They can only make you low crawl for so long,
and the cold, wet mud washed off easy enough.

Nights sucked, but I was only just learning how shitty
it is
to have to get out of warm sleeping bags
on freezing mornings
to a sun that won't help.

The pain of it is cumulative,
and the nine mile hike in the blizzard was grueling, but
Once we began that last stretch
and marched under the
"We Make Marines" arch
I knew I'd made it.

Hiking without warming layers left me wet with sweat-
shivering in the cold, and aching
both physically and emotionally

Standing at parade rest, waiting
The Drill Instructor appeared in front of me and asked
"What does this mean to you?"
I stared through him
with all the Discipline he'd drilled into me
And replied
"Everything."

He put the black Eagle, Globe, and Anchor emblem in my
hand
And shook it
Like a man
And I cried
Like a baby

1.1-11 THE CALL

We had only communicated through flowery love letters.
They probably turned me into a poet
as much as boot camp turned me into a Marine.
After three months I nervously dialed her number,
My heart beat like a war drum against the tone ringing
Angelic voice answered
"Hello?"
To the unfamiliar number
and I answered in a raspy, hoarse
unfamiliar voice.
"Hey babe, it's Mason."
Awkward silence from such surprise
"How are you?" she asked.
...
...
...
"I'm a Marine."
What more was there to say?
We both always knew I would be.
What else was there I could be?
My voice sounded like
"we did it."
Her silence sounded like
"oh, what have we done?"
She knew in her heart
between me, her, and the Corps
this would likely all come undone.
Our relationship would be reduced to
short honeymoons
and long phone calls.
That's it,
That's all.
She was a Queen
and I was a pawn
for answering The Call.

1.2.
BOOT
DROP

1.2-1 LORDS OF THE FLIES ━━━━━━

They call it the infantry because we're child soldiers.
17, 18, 19, yes, I was older,
but they broke me just the same; made us all colder.
They put the weight of the world on our shoulders.
As high school seniors we read "Lord of the Flies,"
Then spent a year dehumanized,
hazed, terrorized.
First by DI's,
then by seniors.
Their job is to fill us with hate, make us leaner,
meaner,
The guns can always be a little bit cleaner.
In the infantry it's not just knowing the knowledge,
It's learning the culture and developing the demeanor.
It's not just mastering the skills,
but accepting the bloodlust
to measure worth by confirmed kills,
Adolescents seeking cheap thrills,
not even responsible enough yet to pay bills,
Yet they ask these same kids to take hills.
We get by on our own savage pride,
our own worst enemies,
ourselves we despise,
Architects of our own demise,
when I checked into the Fleet I realized
We were our very own brand of "Lords of the Flies."

1.2-2 BOOTS

I remember days when it was
"hey boot this and hey boot that."
I thought I was lucky to be a boot in CAAT,
even after Corporal Stoyle threatened me
with a baseball bat.
I saw how the boots in 81s had it bad.
My 31 buddies in Bravo and Charlie Guns
were always tired and sad.
Line company senior 31s were
permanently drunk and mad.
Hazing us like it's our fault
for the combat pump they never had.
Boots with high and tights,
seniors take everything to the high and right,
Put us all in a room, give us gloves, make us fight.
Field days last all night.
Bring on the tourniquet drills
for when the blood spills and
sometimes they just bang on your door
drunk at 3 am for cheap thrills.
Bored, bitter seniors with time to kill.
Testing us, pushing until we all had our fill.
Might makes right,
Seniority grants authority.
Knowledge, they knew more than me
Far more experienced
in the ways of the infantry.
Just a stupid boot, Marine Corps infancy
Lamenting my life,
wishing it was run differently.
They weren't lying when they said Parris Island was only
the beginning,
now I'm doing a police call that seems never ending,
playing fuck fuck games and never ever winning.

1.2-3 ROCK EATER

I'm a Rock Eater
I'm a Heavy Bleeder
I'm a Happy Greeter
To Death's Keepers

I'm a Rock Eater
I'm a Mother Fucker
I'm an Older Brother
I'm a Big Trucker

I'm a Rock Eater
I'm a Non Thinker
I'm a Hard Drinker
I'm the Middle Finger

I'm a Rock Eater
I'm a Hard Hitter
I'm a Lot Thicker
I'm a Brick Shitter

We're Rock Eaters
Yell "GUNS UP!"
Too Fuckin' Tough
We'll Fuck you Up

We're Rock Eaters
We're Horny Breeders
We're Slut Pleasers
We're Ass Eaters
We'll Knock you Up

We're Rock Eaters
Whole Lotta Hate
Whole Lotta Weight
We're Gatekeepers
We're Hatebreeders

I'm a Rock Eater
I'm a Big Dicked
Murder Demon
Fire Breathin'
Coke Fiendin'
Godless Heathen
Rock Eater

1.2-4 BUMS

Weapons Company is full of the Battalion's
Heavy Hitters,
Big Chew Dip Spitters,
Sniper School Never Quitters,
Heavy Guns 31s built like Brick Shitters,
Missilemen with Javelins
heat seeking delivered,
But I must admit
the dirty motherfuckers
with the toughest livers
were the Steel Rain Givers.
Properly called 81s,
AKA the Shady Bums,
AKA the Skatey Ones,
A bunch of fools, but they weren't dumb,
heavy suppression they'll give you some.
Tougher than
Gun Drills uphill,
grab the aiming stakes,
let's shake and bake,
Willie Pete and H.E.
outlawed by the Geneva Convention, ya see.
Boots cried "hazing" and went UA but to me
they were just getting trained
properly,
realistically,
ruthlessly;
No room for your bitching in the infantry.
Especially under the heavy tubes and base plates,
carry the weight to rate to skate,
dug in on gunlines among mortar apes playing spades,
A gang of gun monkeys, fulla hate.
Dirty buncha degenerates,
with the violence and liquor generous,
get rounds on target in a pinch,
no worse enemies or better friends.
Almost no regards for garrison rules or
regulations, but no hesitation
to put the weak in their place and
some say they lack respect for authority
but they run off seniority,
accounting for the majority
of behaving abhorrently,

resulting in good ol' NJP.
Bad attitudes from running the tubes,
a buncha disgruntled dudes
with an unhealthy love of booze.
Circle round the plotting board,
what are these goons plotting for?
81's out of control in
every victor unit in the Corps,
a First Sergeant's worst nightmare
until we all go back to war.

1.2-5 ODE TO AN M240B ——————

A rifleman can build or buy a weapon similar to what he
was issued.
But what of the machine gunner,
and his fully automatic, belt fed, no shit weapon of
war?
What firearm will he ever own or operate again
that can stir the feelings and passion and lust in his
heart?
A bitch to carry and to clean,
that most reliable weapon
of the Marines.
The backbone of the infantry,
Movement without suppression is suicide.
Guns
Six guns cyclic, rolling, talking,
Oh the frenzy
The music
The symphony of fires
Into action, out of action
"RELOADING!"
"BARREL CHANGE!"
"GUN UP!"
Hard leaning shoulder pressure
Dug into the buttstock
Long bursts
"DIE MOTHERFUCKER DIE!"
"DIE! DIE!"
Neuroscientists found that shooting a machine gun
stimulates the same parts of the brain as sex.
Feeding hormones
Chambering dopamine
Firing the neurons
Extracting adrenaline
Ejecting serotonins
And like sex with a beautiful woman,
once in the act, I don't know
where you end
and I begin.

As the gunner becomes a human extension of the machine
gun,
so too does the machine gun
become the mechanical manifestation
of his human will.
All the time spent with the 240 is why
all machine gunners want to do
is Fight, Fuck, and Kill.

1.2-6 CENTENNIAL ———————————

Welcome to the Infantry
1st Battalion, 6th Marines.
What a great time it is, you see...
It's our 100th Anniversary!
A century since Belleau Wood,
we celebrate our Brotherhood!
In gas masks Devil Dogs fought to the death
through machine gun fire
to stab Germans in the chest.
Put on that green service alphas suit.
Tonight we might not treat you like such a boot.
At the ceremony we'll drink the place dry,
at the barracks we'll practice eye for an eye.
What else would we do on this historic night
But have a sprawling three way company fight?

All's well that ends well
and we still laugh
about the night
when a Marine
from Charlie
was beaten
into a coma
with a pipe.

1.2-7 BORN IN A BAR ───────

Alcoholic evenings and liquored nights
give way to caffeinated reveilles
and nicotine fiending duty days.
So many ways we desecrate our
sacred weaponized bodies,
Destruction of government property-
a mockery.
Monsters fueled by Monsters
achieving peak performance.
Behind dead sunken, drunken eyes
Souls are dormant, mental torment.
Thousand yard stare.....
long time since they could care
Spiritual wear and tear
Drowned in spirits
Let's hear it.
Every November 10th
Celebrate yourselves
Born in a Bar
Teufel Hunden, Hellhound Devil Dogs
Looking for the next shot to take
to kill someone for their CAR.

The weight of the M240B is 27.2 lbs
It is an air cooled,
belt fed,
crew served,
fully automatic,
gas operated,
open bolt
weapon system
with a max effective range of 3,725 meters,
an area range of 1,800 meters on tripod
and 800 meters on bipod,
and point range of 800 meters on tripod
and 600 meters on bipod,
but a good gunner can easily hit targets at a grand on
bipods through iron sights.
I was, and I could.

Sustained rate of fire is 100 rounds a minute,
6-8 round bursts,
4-5 second pauses,
barrel change every ten minutes.
Rapid rate of fire is 200 rounds a minute,
6-8 round bursts,
2-3 second pauses,
barrel change every minute.
Cyclic rate of fire is 600-650 rounds a minute,
barrel change every minute.

I remember this information for both
the M2 .50 cal heavy machine gun
and the Mk19 grenade machine gun as well.
I could hit targets almost two thousand meters away
with both of those weapon systems.
The 8 principles of machine gun employment are
PICMDEEP,
which my buddy Drew tattooed on my bicep.
I can still tell you the Classes of Fire
with respect to the Gun, Target, and Ground.
I miss the way my heart raced when I heard
the Cyclic Talking Guns Sound…

but I won't bore you anymore
with what I learned from my homework
assigned by seniors in the Corps.
They made us all write knowledge until our hands were in
knots,
and that was the least severe of the prices paid
in the School of Hard Knocks.

1.2-10 MACHINE

What does it mean to be a Marine?
To give up your color
and become a shade of green.
Can you live a life famished and lean?
Can you thrive in a culture cruel and mean?
Can you laugh at horror
and smile at the obscene?
Can you live and die by a cold steel gun?
Do you have the endurance for resupply runs?
Can you march with combat load in step
to the rhythm of the war drums?
Will you plunge a bayonet
into the chest of a Hun?
Can you suffer in silence
and say it was fun?
Can you do whatever violence
must be done?
Will you kill 'em all until
all the killing is done?
What does it mean to be a Marine?
Meat
for the grinder
to feed
the Machine.

1.2-11 "WHAT'S YOUR 9-LINE?"

It wasn't taught at Infantry Training Battalion,
but the Combat Instructors hinted
We should fucking know it
like our life depended on it.
We all wondered why this piece of knowledge
would be what we were so harshly judged by
upon our arrival.
Once taught, we understood that it was critical
to our survival.
Grid
Call Sign
# of Patients by Precedence
Special Equipment
# of Patients by Type
Security
Marking
Nationality
NBC
Casualties from IEDs get a Golden Hour,
if they even get that much time,
sometimes no one is coming to save you
That's how life goes on the line.
On the catwalk, passing by, if a senior would catch your
eye
"Hey boot, what's your 9-Line?"
What he was really asking you was
"I know how to save your life,
do you give enough of a fuck to learn to save mine?"

1.2-12 READY

Force in Readiness, America's 9-1-1,
anywhere in the world in 72,
For you.
Ready to fight
For you.
Ready to stay up all night, days on end, hallucinating
For you.
Ready to go without food, water, sanitation, comfort,
For you.
Until I simply can't anymore
For you.
Ready to kill
For you.
Ready to lose limbs
For you.
Ready to die
For you.
Only thing I'm not ready to do
is watch my brother do it
For you.

1.3.
SYRIA

1.3-1 USELESS WISHES

Wish I could take back
that night I left.
Headed to the Middle East
off to War to "Secure your Peace."
Sitting on that bus, looking through
the window at you,
My best friend in the window seat, crying,
Looking at his crying kids; 1&2.
And you looking at me
looking at you.
Tears in our eyes,
nothing I could do.
You tightly held my mother's hand
and watched me ship off to The Sand.
These useless memories, these useless wishes,
they haunt me too.

1.3-2 FOREIGN POLICY

We are the Generation
who grew up watching wars.
Our earliest memories are Towers
crumbling down to the ground,
taking 3,000 lives along with ours.
Now that we have come of age we know
The Truth:
America's Foreign Policy is
A pissed off, dirt poor 19 year old kid with a rifle;
hazed for a year by a burnt out, divorced, 21 year old
kid with a machine gun,
and they're just here for the violence.
Politics here are only as conservative or liberal
as our trigger fingers want them to be.
It's ironic that we were instructed to
"Win Hearts and Minds"
because if the ROE weren't so strict
that's right where we'd be aiming,
just like the Failure to Stop drills taught us.

1.3-3 HORIZONS OF HORROR

The long barrels loom
above the horizon,
threatening the world with their
awe inspiring power.
There is something undeniably menacing
about the sight of the gun line
standing in violent contrast to the barren desert.
Artillery answers the Call
For Fire.
They do this almost every half hour
twenty four hours a day.
For many months the artillerymen slave away
performing the horrible work of the cannons.
Oh God, how Howitzers roar.
Thunderous booms report their hatred and discontent
to the Gods of war.
The sun soaks the late evening sky blood red and
the ground shakes in applause.
Your solar plexus rattles in your chest.
Death reigns from above in this world,
in this war.

1.3-4 SYRIAN SUNSETS ———————

"Listen up"
Staff Sergeant slurred at us,
huddled around him in dusty FROGs.
"You're deployed now
and you've gotta get off the tit.
Your girlfriend is gonna cheat on you
anyway...
so just enjoy this.
This is the coolest you're ever gonna be.
You're in someone else's country,
patrolling their streets
with heavy machine guns.
You will never be this badass again.
Make the most of it."
He was right.
I sat on my turret hatch,
many an afternoon
eating chili mac and cleaning my
Ma Deuce
while watching Marine artillery do their horrible work.
Thundering hate through the air
bringing the city of Raqqa to its knees,
and ISIS with it.
Howitzers roared for death and destruction
as the fiery sun
painted a masterpiece
in the wide Syrian sky.
Such beautiful chaos.
I have watched the sun set
in lands both beautiful and austere
since then, and still
my heart misses the desert.

1.3-5 REFUGEE KIDS

Talking heads on TV talk about toxic masculinity,
and pointing and laughing at all of its fragility,
and their feminist rhetoric angers you so,
But maybe they're onto something,
ya know?
Look around at those you see
surrounding you in the infantry.
Consider the root of the word as you grow older.
Infantry is Latin for
"Young Soldier."
What are all of us young men chasing here?
For what
have we sacrificed these precious four years?
What exactly
are we trying to prove?
Is it worth
all that we stand to lose?
Refugee kids in the wake of postmodern American society,
here trying to connect with the ancient warrior ways of
masculinity.
Disappointed by the peacetime infantry.
Does it keep you up at night?
after all you gave to the Corps,
the orphaned refugee kids of Syria
still know more than you about war?

1.3-6 PAINTINGS

If I could paint you a picture, baby,
I would show you what it looked like from the turret.
When you were back at home,
waiting and wondering
where I was or
what I was doing,
but I could never find the words to tell you.
I couldn't find the words to tell myself
Oh, what things I saw.
I'd show you the barren sands;
The Syrian Wastelands.
I'd paint a scene of sunsets and sunrises and the
destruction underneath,
how helpless I felt,
like fever dreams,
one minute cruising along and the next I scream
"WAKEF," but really just begging "PLEASE
STOP, OR I'LL SHOOT!"
I thought I was ready but I was just a boot.
As I cordoned these
IEDs
my head filled with these
possibilities
of explosions and killing these
Syrians over trivialities.

If I could paint you a picture, baby,
I'd show you
what they looked like
in my ACOG sights
400 meters on the BDC
and a wind hold to the right.
You were just waking up a day later when
I got back to the FOB that night
I was angry that I wasn't a killer
so I turned it into a fight.

If I could paint you a picture, baby,
I'd show you the refugee camps,
the orphaned children bathing
naked in the streams like tramps,
Yes I'd show you the displaced far and wide,
I'd show you what it looked like
when I was the lead vehicle gunner
with nowhere to hide.

I'd paint you a machine gun, baby,
and show you how instead of your curvy hips
I held on tight to black spade grips and
this deployment altered my headspace
and ruined our timing,
and all I have left are these words I'm rhyming.
I'd paint you the 50 caliber brass ammunition gleaming
gold in the sun,
I'd show you the 5 miles of the base perimeter of my
daily run
I'd paint you the loaded chamber of my condition one gun
I'd paint a happier ending to our story,
but I only know the one.

1.3-7 I WRITE POETRY, NOT ROE ——————

I don't write the ROEs, I just write my poetry.
I'm not the one who came up with the TEEP.
I don't choose where I deploy or under what sky I sleep.
I am the Tool, not the author of Foreign Policy.
I am an expendable chess pawn in the infantry.
For thousands of miles I patrolled.
and I didn't snatch a single soul.
I stood in a machine gun turret
for thousands of miles
I saw both ISIS glares that didn't dare
and refugee children's smiles.
I still hate the sound
when I admit I didn't fire
a single fucking round.
I came home cold and alone
needing combat suboxone for my
heroin firefight desires.
Rumor was Green Berets had requested our aid
in Raqqa for support by fire,
But the commanding officer had other plans,
he wanted no lives to expire.
For avoiding casualties this man with two degrees
probably awarded a ribbon with a star,
but me and my brothers still feel misplaced shame
because we didn't earn a CAR.
It's taken me years, over many beers and some tears,
to sort through these issues.
I'm thankful now; no guarantees
that flying bullets will miss you.

1.3-8 HOW TO SPOT AN IED ————

Scan left to right,
Look for ant trails and
unusual piles of trash.
It's a war zone, so trash is everywhere.
Instincts give goosebumps that raise hair.
Alone in the turret the responsibility is mine
Establish a baseline
Search for anomalies
Rewired and intended to
Produce casualties
All day every day until
Everything became a pressure plate
and I became the IED.

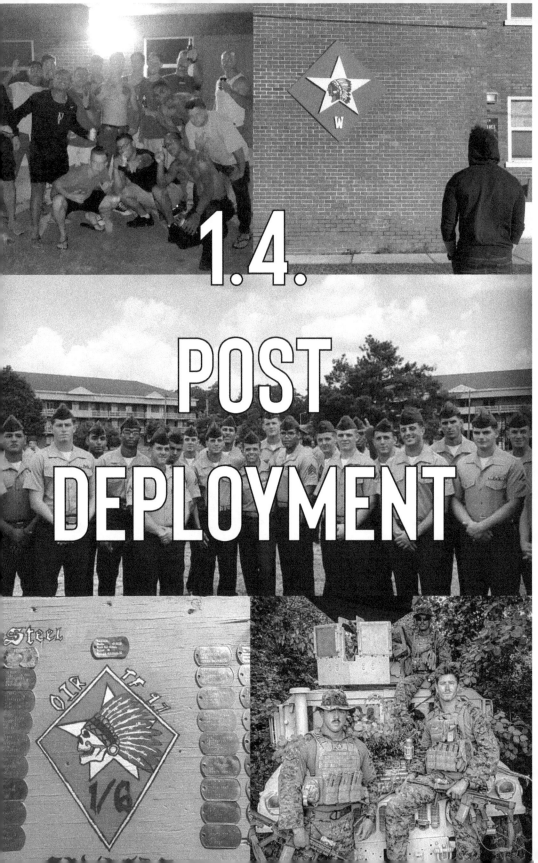

1.4.
POST
DEPLOYMENT

1.4-1 FAR AWAY

Around
Her hair
She wore a yellow ribbon
She wore it
in the springtime,
in the early month of May
She wore it for that young Marine
who's far, far away
One day
He came
Back home from his deployment
He came back in the winter
Right before Christmas Day
In bed
He stared
Holes into the ceiling
In his eyes
she saw
her young Marine
was far, far away

1.4-2 CULTURE

What they don't know is
The Recruiter, the Station, the Bus, that's takin'
us to the Island, the Depot,
no longer people
The lights, on line
Nothing is fine
The DIs
The screaming, the running, the beatings,
the drillings, not eating
The racks, the fights, the packs, the hikes
The letter writing nights

What they don't know is
The fleet, the boots
When they meet
the Seniors
So much fucking meaner
The bricks, the licks, the hazing, the training,
The field when it's raining.
The cold dead eyes, the seven ton rides,
The gun drills, the PT, the family
that never sees me.
The guns, the range, the targets,
The NJP in front of First Sergeant,
The skaters, the tricks, the officer politics,
the kiss ass suck dicks

What they don't know is
the parties, the cookouts,
the brawls, the lookouts
The drinking, the drugs, the cheating, the breakups
and Jody lovin' wives,
the tears from suicides.
The widows, the brothers,
the crying kids and mothers
The bracelets, we hate this

What they don't know is
The Company, the Boys,
enlisted thugs, the goodbyes, the hugs
Deployment, the bus, the plane, the war, the missions
Patrols, the heart, the soul,
the heat, the sweat, the fear
of death
The rush, the hush, the rhythm, the monotony.
It's not about the medals, the ribbons, the blues,
the balls and the views,
the awards that everyone adores.

It's about the unit, the history, the honor, the
violence, the loyalty
Means more to me
The days, the nights,
the rifles, the belt feds,
the seniors, the boots
The 240s rhythm
every time it shoots
The feeling of libo
on early dismissal
The rockets, the mortars, and missiles.
The flaks, packs, and kits,
all of us living this shit.
Go home, alone, the end
You miss your friends,
the platoon, the squad, the team.
The culture of the United States
Infantry Marines.

1.4-3 GEN POP

We are general population
Companies
Battalions
Regiments
of nameless, faceless, expendable
Lance Corporals and PFCS and privates
some of us 2nd awards
and whether we've got our sea service yet or not,
We're all the same in the eyes of the BCs:
900 libo risks he has to tell not to
Drive drunk or
Fight the locals or
Impregnate strippers or
Light government property on fire

Don't be a dick my CO would say
We were a bunch of dicks anyway.
Our forefathers were drafted to carry guns
They sang It Ain't Me,
I ain't no fortunate one.
We all volunteered but it's still true
we're all misfits through and through.
All of us are mostly blue collar and
most of these boys don't know their father.
Society had no place for us so
why would we bother?
White boys, Hispanics, some black dudes too
we were held out from the Melting Pot to become Grunt
Stew
Civilians bitch about equality and racism and fight
But me and my brothers all became equal when we gave up
our rights
No color here, equally worthless shit stains of green
Down here with the Gen Pop Infantry Marines.

1.4-4 BROTHERS

From all over the country, some as young as 17.
Only a few as old and washed up as me.
Young men looking for something,
lost in the postmodern wilderness of bullshit,
Bored, angry, horny hearts longing for violence.
Recruiters like serpents slithering across campuses
with the forbidden apple that almost always
ends with us saying "Fuck the Corps."
None of us knew what we wanted and the lack of knowledge
lead to a lot of
"Pain retains" classes on knowledge of:
How to run
How to gun
How to shoot with intent to kill
How to put on tourniquets when the blood spills.
I watched them deploy with me and grow,
the transition back and forth from field to libo,
Baby faced kids, clowns in the circus of belligerence
and drinking to blackout-
Turned to squad and team leaders, screaming directions
and placing shots perfectly,
Seamlessly transitioning from barracks parties to night
raids,
no loyalty to those afraid.
Where we go one we go all, yell "GUNS UP" for ranges as
well as barracks brawls.
They were all just bastard kids from the same hateful
mother-
I trust them with my life because the Corps made them my
brothers.

1.4-5 THE NIGHT

She asked God every night what she should do,
she prayed "God I love him but he's nothing like you."
She spent her nights sleeping alone
and she anxiously waited for his voice on the phone.
Without her man she stayed out of the bars,
and thought of him sleeping under the stars,
or patrolling through Middle Eastern bazaars,
with green-eyed devils he called his brothers,
other boys lost to the night worried about by their
mothers.
Ever since deployment he'd become short and mean,
spends all night stalking the woods seeing shades of
green,
his nights off at shady bars being obscene.
He burns his candle at both of its ends,
she doesn't think he's ever coming home again.
He's at war with himself that he doesn't want to win.
Hypervigilant insomnia and alcohol have him now,
Wish she could get through to him but doesn't know how.
There's a man stuck under there that she used to love,
but now he's living in sin howling at the moon and the
stars above.
When the news got to her it was worse than she thought.
He was running from his demons and finally got caught.
He called her when he made it home after paying his
bail,
spent the night staring at Satan in a cold county jail.
She could hear it in his voice he'd built his own hell.
All that woman could do was just wish him well,
she'd have better luck tossing quarters in a wishing
well.
Now when she remembers her time with him
she wonders if the Marines own the night
or does the night own them?

1.4-6 HEADSPACE AND TIMING ━━━━━

In love, whether with
A woman or a 50 caliber M2 machine gun,
And in all of life's chance events,
It all comes down to two things:

Headspace
and timing

The headspace, that distance between
The face of the bolt and
The base of the cartridge
Fully seated in the chamber.
That round, poised to complete the mission,
to execute your will on the enemy,
is useless if the headspace is off.
Too much and the firing pin won't strike the primer.
Too little and the whole machine will blow up in your
face.

The timing, so precisely calibrated,
So that the weapon fires while it is recoiling,
is the difference between "gun up" and "dead gunner."

And in life, and love especially,
these things are just as important.
All of my love for you,
packed like gunpowder,
into a belt of ammunition,
Rounds full of good intentions,
fully seated in the chamber,
of our machine gun relationship.

On target at first, at the cyclic rate, running smooth
but,
My headspace did not account for
Distance and Deployment and Depression and Drinking and
The heating and expansion of our lives.

As the misfires came and I charged the weapon,
feeding and ejecting being present,
and I wanting it so badly to work,
I tried to speed up the timing
and it blew up in my face.

"What the fuck?"
The First Sergeant said in enraged disappointment,
demanding to know
The Who, the What and When, the Where, but most of
all....the Why?
I drove my Charger too fast
100-120-140-160
I blasted the music
"Saturday Night" by The Misfits
Because I was crying without her
Saturday night
Because I'm all twisted and reshaped
Into this human extension of
A machine gun
Because the murdered out black as night car roars in
anger
as I stomp the gas to the floor
Like I wanted to scream so many times but didn't
And every time the RPMs maxed out
I let off
and stomped again
Like well timed machine gun bursts
The car lurches forward and slams me back into my seat
I let off
Just so I can stomp again
Each stomp pushes the car faster and faster
I felt the car shaking and I
wanted to know what
hitting that IED felt like,
maybe I wanted to die that night.
Maybe I was the IED.
Adrenaline and manic howls
of guilt and anger in the driver's seat.
Because you ripped me back to America
from the home I found in the sandbox.
Speed is the suboxone
to the heroin combat craving addiction
that ruined my relationship;
Turned me into an animal
couldn't love himself, much less her.
That's what I did in Daytona with a new lust
Fucking the loneliness away
We got in a fight and she kicked me out of her bed,

I couldn't kick the demons out of my head
And that, 1st Sergeant,
is why I got a DUI
in Georgia on the 72.
Because fuck you,
and everything else
That's Why.

SECTION 2: SECOND AWARD SENIOR

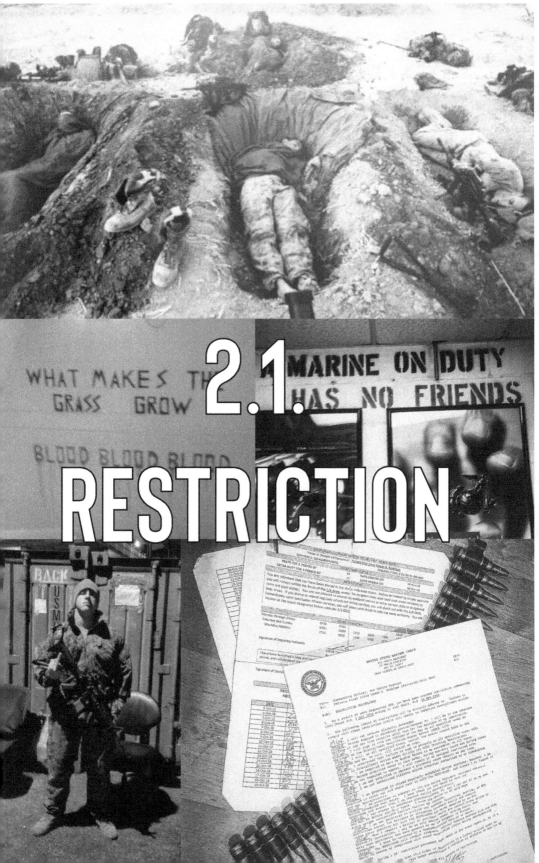

2.1.

RESTRICTION

2.1-1 NON-JUDICIAL

When I needed my command the most
was when they turned their back on me.
I never knew my First Sergeant thought I was the best
Lance Corporal in the company,
until I was at parade rest getting blasted for how he
had to NJP me.
"Yes, I was out of bounds and had no ground to stand
on."
I wish they could've just taken me to the treeline and
put hands on.
"Yes, I was out of bounds going insanely fast."
but normally that's only Company level, not top Brass
RBE with Battalion deployed so the Regiment that doesn't
know me will burn my ass.
The cop said I was drinking, but I refused to blow
so guilty or innocent, who's to know?
Until after they give me a civilian court date, can't
they let it go?
Fuck no.
The Colonel is in Afghanistan so I had to report to the
XO,
With no authority to NJP, but my command didn't know.
I was trembling, barely holding it together as a man,
at parade rest and attention I did stand
as my future was taken by the wave of his hand,
two years later I found out it wasn't even legal-
he was only filling in for the officer in command.
Now I'm a real Marine, 2nd Award,
Damned.
At least he didn't take my money, just my previous rank,
because I still owed a lawyer and bail bondsman
for my night in the drunk tank.
My fate was sealed, it was official,
all I could think was that
"Yes, this punishment feels very Non-Judicial."

2.1-2 ROTTEN APPLE ─────────

Rotten Apple,
Black Sheep.
Reason that my mother weeps.
Cause of all my father's grief.
Promises I never keep.
Dug a fighting hole,
far too deep.
I made this bed,
but I can't sleep.
Lost Rank,
Gained Shame.
The mirror shows
who caused my pain.
Self Loathing
fills my brain.
Lowlife shitbag,
should've been hit by a frag.
Burnt out like a cigarette's drag.
Hide behind the American flag.
"Eat the Apple,
Fuck the Corps."
I don't mean it,
I want more.
Pray they let me
stay for four.
Long night, black sky,
Deep dive,
Don't cry.
I want a war
so I can die.

2.1-3 TEARS

My mother left when I was 12,
taking my two youngest siblings.
Neither could've been older than three,
and that left my father, my little brother, and me.
My father collapsed, wept and cried,
And something in me froze, cracked, and died.
I hugged them both
and told them it would be alright,
I lied to myself
and them that night.
I joined the Marines fourteen years later looking for a
fight,
an unbreakable family of broken boys bonded tight.
Before I deployed my father cried, a sensitive man,
scared I might die.
I was trying to prove I wasn't soft like him.
Although I tried, I must confide, the truth tracked me
down.
I couldn't keep running from my fears,
When life finally broke me, the floodgates released all
the rain
from all those years,
and I still wound up the kind of man who
succumbs to tears.

2.1-4 HEY DOC

Hey Doc,
Can you put me back together?
It's good to have a friend who doesn't have my same
stupid haircut
and gets nautical tattoos.
A friend to all, here to serve the boys who serve.
When I'm broken, and my NCO
doesn't wanna hear it, it is you who
defends my right to not be broken in like battle cattle
with no regard to long term injuries,
my bad back and ankles and knees.
Hey Doc,
can you pour me a glass of Captain Morgan?
because I need to talk...
Yeah, the Company Captain
is gonna make me take that walk.
The NJP is coming
for that drunk joy ride.
I haven't told my parents yet,
But I've thought of suicide.
Hey Doc,
please tell me where the fuck should I go,
my mental pain is a weakness
I don't want other Marines to know.
My broken soul has emotions
that I'm not allowed to show.
So I've come to you Doc,
where else would I go?
You're always at the party,
not just because you bring the IVs,
A Marine needs a specific sailor
when he drifts into rough seas.
You could be Blue Side, kicked up
relaxing in the A/C,
But you chose to come to Green Side
and live in filth with United States Marines.
Greater love hath no man
than to lay down his life for someone else,
Greater love hath no man than Grunts for Corpsman
who protect us from ourselves.

2.1-5 BLOOD

"The needle tears a hole…"
at the plasma donation center.
16 gauge, biggest needle I've ever seen.
Blood pressure cuff constricting, suffocating
my muscular right arm to expose a roadmap of veins.
Sterile and cold and full of
Dirty, Desperate, Impoverished, Unwanted types, and of
course
Marines.
We're poor too, ya know...
Anywhere from thirty to forty dollars
twice a week
to pay the lawyers and court fees.
Force a smile to the nurse
as she drives the needle
into me.
It leaves me hurt,
like a punishment junkie.
I watch all the others in here
on their phones
listening to music
and wonder
"are they rock bottom like me?"
Did the love of their life just tell them
"No, I won't let you
leave me hurt,
again."
I watch the container fill with blood,
thick, red blood.
"Hurt" in my headphones
and gives me chills
as ice cold saline water is forced into me
to replenish lost plasma.

CITATION: TRENT REZNOR

2.1-6 BRICKS

HP 145, 125, 295, 125, 155
are all places I've called home.
The Bricks;
Projects haphazardly centered
around an armory and the CP.
Where the company offices are,
where I checked in with
The Officer of the Day
for 45 days.
Powerlines decorated with boots;
belonged to seniors long gone.
The smoke pits where we burn butts
and bitch
and chug energy drinks
to fight off the hangover from
last night's rager where
we blacked out and damaged government property.
Maybe we
punched tiles out the ceiling
Or
ripped the water fountain from the wall
Or
Fist fought each other
Or maybe
even fought the duty;
Fuck the duty.
Our sense of duty has landed us
in these four walled cells
of black mold and concrete
Bricks.

2.1-7 SUICIDAL-MEMBERS' GROUP LIFE INSURANCE (SGLI)

They creep into your head
They whisper in your ear
They say you're better off dead
But you don't want to hear

These thoughts are not my own
These thoughts come when I drink
These thoughts chill me to the bone
Why is this the way I think?

Evil voices in my head
dwell on my mistakes
Evil voices in my head
It's more than I can take

At night I chain smoke cigarettes
Until the voices stop
It keeps me awake, filled with regrets
And still they never stop

My heart is broken
I only know "alone"
I don't even deserve
to be welcomed back to my home.

I don't know how to handle the guilt
I'm drowning in my shame
King of the empire of shit I built
I alone am the one to blame

Conversations with demons urge me
To move this thing along
Swallow the gun and pull the trigger
Who will miss me when I'm gone?

I probably would've done it by now
Even though I don't want to die.
The only thing that ever stops me
is knowing my Mom won't get the SGLI.

2.1-8 DIG

Deep in the ground
Fighting hole has become my grave
collapsing on all sides.
Honor, Courage, Commitment
Failure
to live and die by the core values
that the Corps tells you it values.
I dug this hole, I gave away
every part of myself
to become a Marine
to become a grunt.
Alcohol and
isolation and
depression and
loneliness and
violence and
bad decisions and
everything expected of us.
They wouldn't give you a good conduct award if
they thought you'd behave.
"Not a real Marine til you've been NJP'd,"
Chesty said.
The stereotype is to self destruct
when you become a human extension of your weapon system
and the Corps aims it at nothing.
The aimless grunt aims it at himself
and kills his own weak thoughts via
well aimed shots of hard liquor.
Not such a hard motherfucker now
Are you, grunt?
They taught you how to dig in,
never how to dig out.
The only way out is through
the hard truths and answers in you.
Start digging.

2.1-9 FAILURE TO CYCLE ───────

Anxiety, buzzing loudly inside of me, like a hive of
bees,
Or a swarm of yellowjackets,
Wound up tighter than a full magazine of full metal
jackets,
Overgassed mind malfunctions,
Tap it and rack it

BANG

Toss and turn in my rack and,
Mind racing, the time and space
between missing the target,
Facing the fact that
I'm a spent shell casing, discarded.
Silence is deafening,
the tinnitus in my ears rings,
Pace the room like a hornet
looking for something to sting.
Hypervigilant hyperventilating,
Thrill seeking behavior so titillating.
Anxiety heightens sensitivity, alcohol numbs and stops
the inhibiting,
Rage increases reactivity, depression and regret follow,
Oh, the futility-
Self sabotage cycle fueled by fragility.

BREATHE

Calm down, write down and unload the saved rounds,
Sink or swim, didn't drown,
Found ways through much darker days,
Weathered hurricanes and storms, failure to cycle not
outside of the norm.
You were taught how to respond and perform.

Immediate and corrective actions:
Observe, tap it and rack it,
Get the gun up and back in action.
Fixing a life requires deliberate actions.

Slow is smooth, Smooth is fast,
Hard men outlast hard times that always pass.

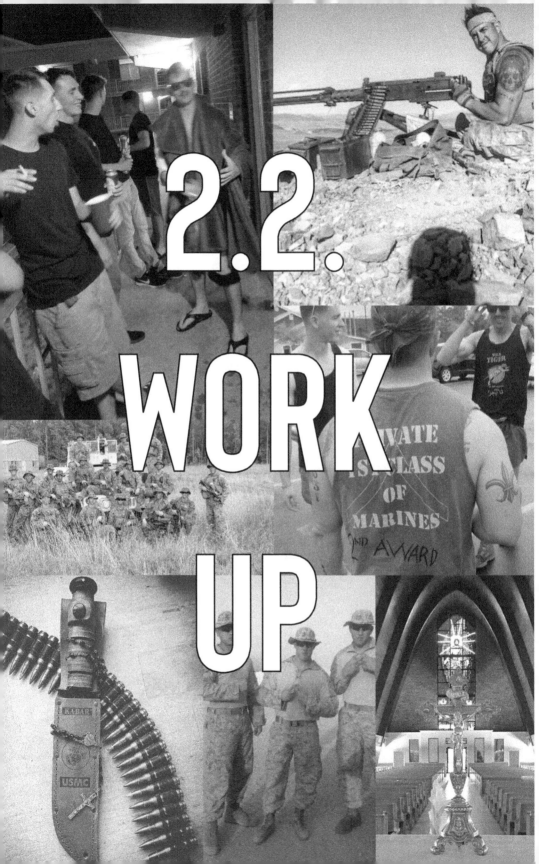

2.2.
WORK
UP

2.2-1 DANGEROUS JACKASSERY ——

The Marine Corps Times called it "Dangerous Jackassery."
I called it the University of Hard Knocks and
we were working on Master's Degrees.
They teach these boots
weapons, tactics, and patrolling at ITB,
but they've got a lot more
Hard lessons to learn to make it in our infantry.
This job is unlike any other employment,
They'll be treated like boots, same as us, until their
first deployment,
and what journalists call "dangerous jackassery"
we see as the fine art of mastering finding enjoyment
in a profession of misery.
They claim that after the Crucible there are no more
initiations,
but boot camp only teaches Drill,
and we have to turn these boots
into kids that want to kill.
Nobody needs to see what goes on
in tree-lines or behind closed doors
to get their sons ready to die in a war.

Please, leave the "Dangerous Jackassery" to me,
and go back to the safety of your shitty magazine.
Keep selling the public the propaganda about the Honor
of these dangerous jackass Marines.

2.2-2 FUCK

Fuck Field Day and Fuck First Sergeant,
Fuck the Range,
Fuck the Pit,
Fuck pulling these targets.
Fuck Corporal What's His Nuts, he's fucking retarded.
Fuck my LT he's an arrogant boot,
Fuck these entitled kids that were just recruits.
Fuck this weak ass hazing charge from my boots.

None of us are getting CARs,
Let's black out at the bricks
Fuck going to a bar.
Fuck Toby's, those broads ain't worth the cover charge.

Fuck the next boot drop
as hard as we're getting fucked
on this field op.
The whole battalion is out here without water,
everyone has hypothermia,
but we still won't stop.

I don't even know what I'm training for anymore,
Completely lost touch with the misguided reasons I
enlisted for.
I became the Rotten Apple that says
"Fuck the Corps."

2.2-3 BLACKOUT AND VOMIT ━━━━

30 racks, Tall Boys, Forty ounces too
Coors, High Lifes, Natty Lights
I need cheap domestic brews.
SHOTGUN! SHOTGUN! Chase me shot for shot!
Gimme that 5th of Jameson,
dark bottle fulla sin,
I'll chug the Venom hot.
Funnel a six pack from third deck
thirty feet below
open up your drunken throat
and give the beer somewhere to go.
Funnel a six pack from third deck
cold beer runs off down your neck
had a drinking problem since I said goodbye to DIs
and their Quarterdecks.
Drink until I'm Fuckin wrecked,
Booze wastes my whole check.
Plastered past the point of no return,
bum cigarettes to watch shit burn,
Jameson comes back around
Yes, I'll take another turn.
We rage against the machine that owns us
and we party fucking hard
Lejeune barracks give us cancer
so we tear the bricks apart.
I got mistakes I want to forget about
so I guzzle alcohol until I black out
lose control of my emotions
fight and scream and cry and shout.
Shepherd offered me muscle relaxers
now I'm fucked up on it.
Blacking out and passing out
and waking up to violently vomit.

2.2-4 INTERNAL ━━━━━━━━━━━━━━━━━━

The wind suddenly picked up
by about five miles an hour and it was
a little too cold for June in Lejeune.
Black as fuck clouds came out of nowhere
Low and fast
You could smell the rain coming
on day two of the ten day field exercise.
The Devil whispered in his ear
"You're not strong enough to withstand the storm"
and Parsons laughed back and said
"Dude, I'm so fucking Internal."

2.2-5 REVEILLE

There are many nights where we meet in my dreams.
Everything fades away;
I develop a lack of peripherals
and lose the situational awareness
that used to take my focus off you.
No sadness,
No pain,
as if I'm not asleep under a tarp
in pouring rain.
I dream as if it's all just
been a bad dream,
as if freezing cold field training,
misery and heartache
was all just a figment of my imagination.
The warmth of your loving embrace,
home in each other's arms,
gives my soul cause for celebration.
And just when I find peace of heart,
and this, like reality seems...
the firewatch sounds Reveille,
and I have to get accountability
for my fire team.
My living nightmare kills
my peaceful dream.

2.2-6 BALLAD OF CORPORAL JOSELOVE –

All you goodie two shoes boots
come and Sit, Kneel, Bend
Gather round me and hear this story
from beginning to the end.
This is the Ballad of "Jose" Joselove,
an RO thug.
Harder than the impact
of a shotgun slug.
A hard charging Corporal that popped for drugs
and was shown no love.
Jose was a competitive son of a bitch
so he took the Recon contract option
to scratch his warrior itch.
The Recon contract ain't always what it seems,
those who don't read fine print
are a recruiter's wet dream.
Jose found himself in over his head
out where the breakers roar.
Just the beginning of the Corps,
pulling him farther from the shore.
In the end he didn't make it
but in life it's all in how you take it.
Jose refocused and kept calm,
went to radio school in Twentynine Palms,
learning to get Comms for bombs.
Jose was determined to only fail once
and make his mark when he finally
made it to the Grunts.
Attached to the Heavy Mortars 81s,
Belligerent and Shady Bums
the Battalion's hardest skating sons.
Base plates and spade tattoos;
hate filled seniors hazing him
afternoons and evenings too,
turned him into a savage dude.
Unfortunately, also got him heavy into booze.
Anything an 03 could do he could do it better.
When everyone's internal and the field ops get wetter,
Jose laughs at the weak crying about the weather.
Jose crushed ruck runs for fun
wanted nothing more than to live by the gun.
Jose loved the infantry but hated soul crushing
garrison,

wasting life in the barracks and
all of his aggression
and a spiraling depression
lead to a transgression
where he broke his hand in a
drunken barroom scrap session.
He had to sit out injured from ITX,
pay attention to what happens next:
Jose at his rock bottom,
thought the whole thing was a joke,
and drunk off his ass he tried a little coke,
popped on the drug test,
and that was all she wrote.
Wasted away for what felt like eternity,
hating life in the RBE.
Lawyers pushing to fight the case,
but this ain't a fairytale, ya see?
Eventually took the NJP
and got out a Terminal Lance in infamy.
He may sound like a shitbag to you,
but I sing you this ballad because that's not true.
Jose was one of the hardest Marines that I ever knew,
so if it can happen to him it can happen to you.

2.2-7 BELT FED ROSARIES

Maw Maw Anna, from Thibodaux, Louisiana.
Anna-Louise Battaglia Rodrigue;
What a beautiful name for a beautiful woman.
I remember fondly,
sleepovers with the cousins,
and going into you and Gerard's bedroom excitedly to
wake you.
No breakfast with Paw Paw
until you'd both finished your rosaries.
So many to pray for,
we were only a few then, but eventually
there were thirteen of us.
First grandson,
you hoped I'd be the Pius One.
I suppose I did spread Christianity,
along with Democracy,
from the barrel of a machine gun.
I got the Chi Rho tattooed over my heart
before deployment.
I suppose the Middle East was safer for Catholics, until
our government decided they were done with it (For now).
I wasn't cut out to be a priest,
but at least,
I got to sit with you in the front row
of our church in my dress blues.
The service uniforms made you smile,
and we didn't have to discuss the trouble
I'd gotten into meanwhile.
Thankfully in the pictures I sent
you didn't understand what
my rank decreasing
as my ribbons were increasing meant.
I was hell-bound and you were heaven-sent.
I probably wouldn't have made it through
if you and Grammy Mert
didn't pray the rosary for me
as cyclic as my 240 ate belts of 7.62.

2.2-8 DRESS BLUES ────────────

Maw Maw, Maw Maw, can't you see?
What the Corps has done to me?
88 years you passed away,
I'm home for your funeral today.
Gentle woman, pillar of community
The whole town is here to see.
Dad and Uncles said for you
I should stand in my Dress Blues.
Standing in line at your wake,
all the hands I had to shake.
Folks that watched me grow up strong,
Now they think I do no wrong.
For my service they all thanked me,
Impressed I joined the infantry.
For my service they all thanked me,
But if only they could see.
Behind all of this patriotism,
is a struggle with alcoholism.

They ask how long I've been in,
then they ask where all I've been.
I mention Syria to awkward silence
and I still fantasize about violence.
To you I represent integrity,
My ex just sees infidelity.
I smile and say it's my honor to serve,
an imposter with a lot of nerve.
Then I stood up to give her eulogy,
not allowed to weep for her memory.
In uniform you can't be yourself,
you're a symbol pulled down off a shelf.
You represent the men that died,
You have to represent with pride.
Your emotions are ripped and torn,
The heaviest thing you've ever worn.
When I took my Dress Blues off
I found myself at a loss.
That night I guzzled a fifth of Crown
and beat my little brother down.
In shame I wept uncontrollably,
My soul belongs to the USMC.
Maw Maw, Maw Maw can't you see?
What the Corps has done to me?
What the Corps has done to me?

She was always surprised to see me
when I walked into the nursing home with my father.
He was there faithfully, daily,
most of every weekend,
caring for his mother,
his own life on hold.

"Mason!"
She'd say in surprise, like I was doomed to never
return.
"I didn't know you were coming in!"

If my father had told her yesterday I was coming to
visit
she'd have forgotten before I showed up.
The days were all blended together to her.
This was her wheelchair bound purgatory,
five years waiting to be reunited in death with the love
of her life.

"How are the Marines? They treating you rough?"
I held her hand and leaned in closely so I could hear
her, and her me.
"Yes Maw Maw, it's rough, but not too bad."

"How long are you here?"
"Just for two weeks for Christmas Maw Maw. I'll be here
to visit as often as I can."
"How are you and your girlfriend?"
"Oh Maw Maw....
we had to break up....
about a year and a half ago now....
it was for the best…"
"That's so sad. I thought she was so good for you
Mason."
"I did too, Maw Maw, I did too."

"Mason,"
she'd ask, about to cry, her old voice breaking,
"Are you still going to church?"

"Yes Maw Maw," I'd say.

I wasn't lying, but I also wasn't explaining
that we prayed to John Basilone
and the gods of Guadalcanal and Belleau Wood,
that our wine was actually blood
and our bread was from a plastic MRE bag.
I didn't explain that we religiously recited
machine gun condition codes
as novenas to Chesty Puller and Smedley Butler.
I didn't tell her that my rosaries
consisted of counting 5.56 NATO rounds
pushed one by one into magazines.
I didn't explain to her that
warfare had become my religion,
and the Marine Corps,
my Holy Universal Church.

"I'm so proud of you, Mason"

Her weak, old, arthritic hand squeezed mine
with all the dying strength it had left.

"Thank you Maw Maw."
I kissed her forehead

"PEACETIME"

It was called "Peacetime."
War was everywhere.

Syria had been in a state of civil war since my junior
year,
ISIS, in a vacuum, established a Caliphate of fear,
from Aleppo to Mosul, and they even brought it here.

It was called "Peacetime."
War was everywhere.

North Korea constantly makes nuclear threats,
China owns us via trillions in debt,
at least we haven't lost Afghanistan….yet.

It was called "Peacetime."
War was everywhere.

There was Russian aggression in the Ukraine,
Genocide in Yemen, leaving nothing but blood stains,
Hamas and Israel at it again, just the same
as it's always been.

It was called "Peacetime."
War was everywhere.

I spent New Year's Eve 2020 in a hospital
with my grandmother and Dad
as Iran rained rockets
on Marines in Baghdad.
My father said "we should go to war."
without considering what his son next to him
was fighting for anymore.

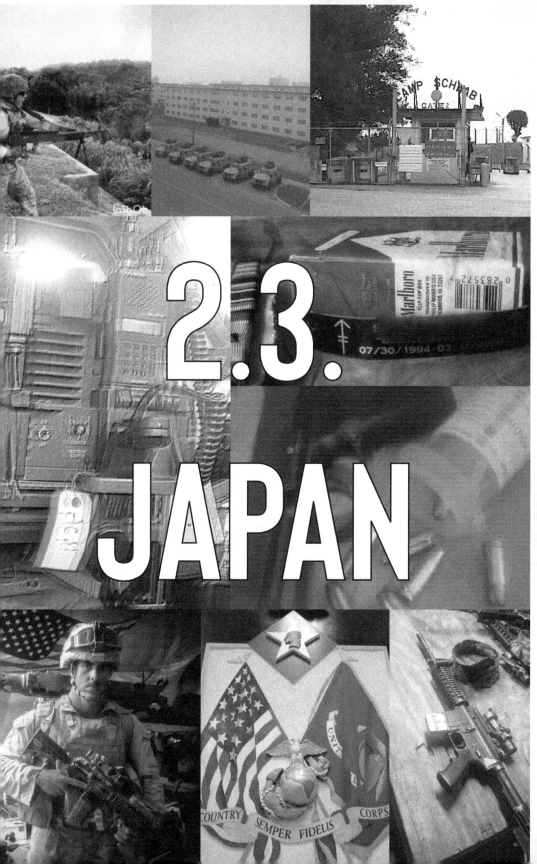

2.3. JAPAN

2.3-1 STANDING BY

Standing by,
Staged,
Main packs, sea bags, deployer bags,
Covered and aligned,
8 hours prior.
Coffee in the battalion classroom
with the families.
Desert cammies and a shaved head
for a war.
Standing by
for seven tons
to load the packs.
Standing by for buses.
You were standing by my side last time.
I, crying on the bus holding my
best friends hand while he cried
watching his babies and wife cry
as they stood by.

This time I stand by in the cold,
warming layers packed for sunny Japan.
Same scene at the barracks,
Marines with their kids and wives and lovers,
holding on tight for
One Last Caress.
This time my hands are in my pockets,
Standing by
myself this time.

Unit Deployment Program to a tropical island,
"forward deployed"
and protested by the Okinawans.
The 4th Regiment Colonel wasn't brief
during his condescending Welcome Aboard Brief
"Oldest and Proudest"
he bragged with so much arrogance
about his regiment,
founded in 1911 to support operations in Mexico,
never even made it there,
surrendered the colors in WWII,
Only Marine Regiment ever to do so...
"Hold High the Torch" you say?
Most of your history "forward deployed" you say?
Sir, the Corps won't let you base your headquarters on
American soil,
so Okinawa is where you toil.
1st, 2nd, and 3rd have all certainly served with pride,
but the torn up colors in WWII is why foreign land is
where you reside.
From where I sit, in my estimation,
this is a military sponsored vacation.
You can cling to "Hold High the Torch,"
but I can see the beach from my barracks back porch.
My Sergeant Major said it's "not a real deployment,"
and most of us don't feel like
real grunts without real employment.
For a wannabe fighting man
that's had a little taste of the desert sand,
It's real hard to get your rocks off in a prefecture of
Japan.
My forefathers killed and died for this rock With the
Old Breed,
So how can I serve with pride if there's no chance to
bleed?
We should all be thankful to get out and say none of our
boys died,
But I theorize that shame from lack of combat
contributes to the spike in suicides.
Okinawans can't you see,
We don't want to waste our time here either on this UDP.

2.3-3 WHEREVER YOU GO ────────

Set out to be your own romanticized hero,
the sum of all your ideas equal to zero.
Set out to be all that you can be,
the Few, the Proud, the Infantry.
You will be both the recruit,
and the hateful DIs.
You will be both the boot,
and bitter senior with sunken eyes.
You will be both the swelling of pride,
and all you despise.
We are the architects of
our success and demise.

You'll travel around the world
and never make it very far.
You'll realize that wherever you go
There you are.

2.3-4 BROKEN AND UNREADABLE ━━━

Yeah, we still talk...
Sometimes
It's very casual and friendly
Can't convey much else and
it's nice to stay in touch because
I'm happy to see how great she's doing,
pursuing her own dreams
instead of abandoning them
to come to Camp Lejeune for me.
That lets me know letting her go
was the right call,
and she can tell I've grown too;
not drinking as much.
Let go of a lot of toxic bullshit, but
Whenever I ask
"Maybe when I get out of the Marines...
we could try again?"
Our comms become
Broken and Unreadable.

2.3-5 BLACK BRACELETS —————————

You hit the fleet as a stupid boot and you
wanna be salty like seniors.
You want long hair and
tattoos and
Caffeine dependence and
Nicotine addiction and
Black bracelets
Because they have all that
until
You get all that.

2.3-6 FAILURE TO STOP

I have fired tens of thousands of rounds
and missed them all.
Every shot so accurately off the mark.
Despite how hard I've tried not to,
I've missed you.
Hits me, sometimes, center mass;
two in the chest.
At such painfully powerful terminal velocity,
penetrates my plates of hate.
My armor breaks, shatters, heart splatters;
What's the matter?
Heartbreak escapes exit wounds waking up
from dreams of you in my empty room.
Full moon, lonesome night, cold bed,
lands a kill shot to the head,

I was at war with myself
when I should've been at home with you.
Yes, these trajectories bisect with these
hearts that bleed at such velocity.
Wake up to reality
Failure to Stop loving you
brings me to my knees,
done everything but beg, "please."
"No", through my heart rips
like NATO green tips.
Never again to caress your hips.
Never again to kiss your lips.
Of all the shots I've taken,
it is you that I missed.

2.3-7 KILL YOUR HEROES ————

Reenlistment rates are low because
Hard charging NCOs
Experience a rude awakening
When they realize that
the Marines that invaded Iraq,
that they grew up idolizing
are the same First Sergeants and Sergeant Majors
Presiding over their NJP for
"Hazing."
I guess the ones we idolized all got out.

Sometimes I have a hard time telling the BC "No"
because of how he charged the enemy
with a SAW and got a Silver Star,

Sometimes I feel guilty,
like I'm letting my First Sergeant down.
Rumor is he killed insurgents
in Fallujah
with an M9.
I was nobody after my NJP,
and I didn't want to be
put back on this pedestal,
I didn't work hard for
awards or boards,
and I'm tired of the guilt trip reenlistment talks.
No matter how many times I sit across from Sergeant
Major
and wish they'd respect my "no"
I still can't kill my heroes.

2.3-8 CUT THROAT CORPS ——————

You can stop blowing smoke up my ass,
I've spent enough time in the field
to spot the snakes in the grass.
I'm not power hungry enough
for your Cut Throat Corps.
There's no more war
so I'm only giving you four.
There's nothing you can offer
I'd stick around for.
My outbound interview is over.
I'm heading out the door.

2.3-9 SILENT KILLER

Inherited the Silent Killer;
Hypervigilant Hypertension.
Anxiety still looking for
the IED.
Bleeding art from
time bomb heart.
I am the IED;
The Killer is me.

2.3-10 PILLS HARD TO SWALLOW ———

I have bad dreams where she's dating a poet now,
But not like me, he's
Classically Trained and in touch with
his Feminine Side
Didn't find his words in the wreckage.
He's not so rough around the edges
that it hurts her to hold him...
"Doc,
The pain is right under the pectoral line and slightly
left of center...
Feels like someone put a pistol
to my heart
and shot it empty."
Heartbroken Hypertension.

She is the nurse at my bed at 3:00 AM.
She chides me for not watching my blood pressure.
"Silent Killer" she says.
The "Killer" is me.
She hears my heart cry out for her
through her stethoscope,
she can prescribe nothing
except for honesty.
Brutal truths make pills hard to swallow.
I ask if she's happier
with a gardener in a war
than a warrior in the garden.
She asks why she'd need something
as useless as a warrior in peacetime,
and reminds me I was only ever
at war with myself.

2.3-11 OKINAWAN SUNSETS

The sunset was beautiful today
and so were you
The colors so vibrant, every shade and hue
as vibrant as your smile
your energy and spirit too.
The gold in the sky like the gold in your hair,
the summer breeze softly surrounds me,
Like when your love was my air.

The clouds soften the pink and orange skies,
just like when we would kiss,
and I would soften your green eyes.
Darkness comes and the sun sets
bringing heartache and sad regrets.

Where does the sun go
when it sets in the sky?
Where did our love go
when it went away to die?

The tides come and go
with the gravity of the moon-
It's pale beauty reflects you
and makes my heart swoon.
I see your face in all the night's stars,
cold and alone I wonder where you are.

I'm so lonesome, I could cry
I'm so lonesome, I could die
I remember warmer days,
Long ago and far away-
When the sun painted the sky a beautiful hue
But the sun is gone now,
and so are you.

2.3-12 SMOKE EM IF YOU GOT EM ———

Smoke 'em if you got 'em.
Bum one if you don't.
My mother says "take care of yourself"
but we both know I won't.
I used to not need nicotine,
not really big on dip,
but I started smoking Ardens in Syria
after we relieved 3/6 on the rip.
I could blame it on the boredom and monotony,
but that would be a lie.
You might think it's because of
the stress and paranoia that I might die.
Truth be told it's none of these things
because it wasn't really that bad.
Deployment was some of the best times
any of us have ever had.
I switched to Camels on my second workup,
my second deployment Marlboro Reds.
I liked smoking in the field with the boys
and there's not much left to be said.
No, Truth be told it's because I'm a deviant
who likes things that are bad for me...
Like dark haired divorcees and driving too fast
and binge drinking until I can barely see.
I like the inhale burn in my throat,
the menthol cool on the exhale out.
I like to smoke alone now,
can't stand when company shows up
with nothing worth talking about.
It's not a chemical thing,
whenever I want I could easily quit,
but I get a strange peace
when I time the sunset
with the cigarette's final hit.
So smoke 'em if ya got 'em,
Bum one if ya don't.
My mother says I should start living right,
but we both know I won't.

2.3-13 AIN'T WHAT IT USED TO BE ━━━

These old knees just
ain't what they used to be,
when I could run the PFT
fastest in the Company.
Pullups, at least twenty three,
hundreds of crunches like a breeze.

But this old back just
ain't what it used to be
from years in the infantry.
Humped for eternity
rifles, tripods, two-forties,
sometimes Ma and Mark nineteens.
Step it out, rhythmically,
marching breaks us physically.
Mentally, it's misery,
but crying in futility
makes you look full of fragility.
So suck it up silently.
That mileage took quite a toll on me,
ankles, back, hips, and knees,
Basically neck down you see.

Don't want to sound dramatic, but
there's fire in my sciatica.
Now I don't feel so tough;
like I didn't do enough.
Other generations had it rough
and they all keep telling me
"Son, the Corps ain't what it used to be."

WITNESS ME

In this world of false idols and hypocrites
preaching fake philosophies and phony dichotomies.
Selling the masses lies and cookie cutter lobotomies,
fulfilling history's repeating prophecies.
I just want my truth to set me free,
who am I when no one is left to tell me who to be?
The Marine Corps took the best of me.
I'm freely giving anyone who will listen what's left of
me.

I write prolifically.
I pace restlessly.
I drink excessively.
I hate incessantly.
I think aggressively.
I freeze, breathlessly.

I am anxiety, don't stand next to me.
I am a problem, deployment exacerbated me.
I am an IED, detonate me.

Never comfortable with peace or silence.
I wanted the speed, the chaos, the violence.

In case things are going too well:
Break the glass,
Foot to floor,
Spare no gas,
Die young, Live fast,
I'm spent casings,
I'm only brass.

2.3-15 TRAILER PARK

Jacksonville,
I just checked in
to the Triangle Motor Inn,
To see what condition
your condition was in.
Den of filth and sin.
I write poetically, and hope desperately
this doesn't sound like poetry.
Yes, you whore, you know it's me,
back again, can't get enough of trying to get back
the years of my life you took from me.

The old Marine Corps cadence
about having a gal in New Orleans,
balancing her and you tore me in two,
like jeans ripped at the seams.
All those years of sleepless nights in the woods and
lucid dreams,
living like savages with the gun teams.

Through the skies, the Ospreys fly,
New River flows to Onslow Beach,
Like the tears lovers cried
in this junk town where love comes to die.
You offered nothing but barber shops and booze,
Strip clubs and cheap tattoos,
I could barely afford my own Dress Blues.

Prison block barracks where I learned to sing the blues,
four fucking years I paid my dues.
Jackson Vegas, I fucking hate you,
Hate was the only thing
you taught me to do.
You white trash trailer park,
littered with shattered lives and broken hearts.
Neon lights illuminate your sins
in this city so dark.

2.3-16 ALWAYS FAITHFUL ─────────

I saw toddlers cry uncontrollably
when their fathers got on a bus to deploy.
I saw a Sergeant who normally
showed no emotion cry
after watching his first daughter born
over a zoom call in Syria.
I saw wives take the kids and leave
their husbands in empty base houses.
I saw wives kick their husbands out
and make them couch surf.
I saw my Platoon Sergeant,
who was like a father to us,
miss all four of his own son's birthdays
and his anniversary for field exercises.
My First Sergeant told us
he hadn't seen his son in a year
when our flights got delayed indefinitely,
To share with us that we
are all going through it together.
I saw families torn apart
and swallowed whole
by the Marine Corps.
I saw it crush the hearts of men
who realized what they were really sacrificing.
I saw them show up to work
every day
in spite of it all,
Without an ounce of self pity.
Even the men who cheated on their wives
were Always Faithful.

2.3-17 UNSUSTAINABLE RATE ————

I ran cyclic for four years,
It took a thirty rack of beer to get me to sleep,
adding liquor lead to angry outbursts and shattered
glass
before I collapsed in a drunken heap, to weep.

It took a pot of coffee and a few cans of Monster every
morning to get me going.
Hungover at PT I sometimes fell out,
often felt shame and self loathing about
cyclically getting loaded and unloading,
my body and soul eroding,
when the barrel gets hot
they think I might end up imploding,
Headspace and timing was off
and I wound up exploding.

All my love turned to hate,
I ran at the unsustainable rate,
I took a sledgehammer and swung at fate,
The handle broke from the weight,
I broke my hands punching my own death's gate.

I ran cyclic until I burnt out,
I tried to scream but had no breath to shout.
I gave everything I had without a doubt,
but what do I do when the linked 7.62 ran out?

Doc took my pack and said
"Buddy, buddy, it'll be okay,"
It was only notional anyway.

2.4.
TERMINAL
LEAVE

2.4-1 ENDEX

I remember nights through PVS14s
The woods washed in eerie green
We Own the Night
U.S. Marines

Maintain visual with the rest of the team
Squads patrol through my dreams
Sleepless Nights
U.S. Marines

Year after Year, Month in Month out,
Op after Op, LZ Dodo, Combat Town,
know these woods inside and out,
Rack out under starry nights as
U.S. Marines

Panic washes over me in my
barracks room
Nevermore to step off with the boys under a full moon
Never thought I'd miss my kit,
or give a shit
Typical of U.S. Marines

Nobody likes to say it quite so blunt,
How we'll miss these woods and living as grunts
Hunters in the night, training for a fight,
U.S. Marines

In the cold and the rain
And the mud and the pain
All for the moral high ground that we gain
U.S. Marines

We suffer the most just so we can boast
We're tougher than you,
you know it's true
Just make sure you don't have any regrets
When you realize you've heard your final

ENDEX

Forevermore yet Nevermore…U.S. Marines

STANDARD ISSUE

The Crown Royal had cut us,
pouring our trauma all over the bedroom,
Hateful words spilling out of her mouth
"You think you're special but
piece of shit Marines like you are a dime a dozen."
How dare she insult my ten cent squad.
"Such a mean thing to say" I thought at the time,
but it feels so true here in the CIF turn in line.
Tarp, poncho liner, whole sleeping system too
weren't warm enough to get me through
cold nights I should've spent with you.
Main pack cracked and weathered and torn,
salt stains on the plate carrier kit I had worn.
Gore Tex I wore to try and stay dry in the rain
some of the only gear I didn't have to wash to get out
the stain,
from field op interruptions of my barracks nights
drinking my pain.
Looking at all my gear wondering if I'd do it all over
again...
Knowing what I know now, would I somehow
have chosen a path that didn't place this kevlar over my
furrowed brow?
I smile, turning in my canteens and canteen cup,
remembering all the cold mornings
spent drinking cowboy coffee with the boys after waking
up.
Reveille got the best of me and the Corps took the rest
of me,
turning in everything except for my boots,
it feels like just yesterday I was only a recruit.
Another cliche enlistment, maybe her words cut true.
Looking at my gear all over the floor
maybe I was standard issue too.

2.4-3 RIBBON STACK ──────────

We tell our stories on our chest,
Mine does not look like the rest.
There are some who after ribbons chase.
National Defense is where we start the race.
After those first thirty shitty days as a boot in the
fleet,
You'll get your GWOT as a treat.
After your workup you'll finally deploy and get that Sea
Service,
Now you're a Senior, boy!
That's the minimum everybody's got these days,
except I went somewhere that gave
"Combat" Pay
And everyone asks why I have that one with a star,
It's for hanging out in Syria for two phases of OIR.
And once we got IPAC to give a fuck, they let us wear a
Gold-bordered JMUC.
And I get questions from near and far
about how my deployment "doesn't count"
because we didn't get a CAR.
But what really makes everyone think
My stack is a scam;
I'm a three and half year Lance with
no Good Cookie and two NAMs.
I like the colors and shine on my rectangular rack,
but I want you all to know that we are all
so much more than our ribbon stack.

2.4-4 FLAGS OF OUR BROTHERS ——————

It cost $18.99, tax free,
the last thing
I'd ever buy at that PX.
New, vibrant,
arterial, lifeblood red,
like a four year hemorrhage.
Golden tassel fringe around the three by five foot
perimeter, securing my perfect
Eagle, Globe, and Anchor.

It was Friday, waiting on Battalion formation
for post deployment leave, five days before I got out on
Terminal Leave.
Began with a small idea: a corner for each company, a
spot for each Weapons platoon.
I made my rounds, gave my hugs, took my pictures, said
my goodbyes,
and one by one my brothers signed.
Inside jokes and well wishes, good memories and deep
laughter
distracted the fact that
we may never see each other again.

My last Battalion formation, light drizzling rain,
The last time I'd ever stand amongst
the masses of men I'd come to call family.
I had the bold idea to take this flag into the company
office,
so my command could sign it too.

I may not always have agreed with
everything they did, and at times this is
a Cut Throat Corps, but
I worked for my heroes.
My Platoon Sergeant, then
First Sergeants and Gunnies, Captains and Majors,
even BC and the Sergeant Major
all took their time to honor me,
the messages written so humbling.

That night in an altered state of mind I read each name,
each message.
I laughed.
I cried.
I wrapped myself up in it and felt the love
and brotherhood
and loyalty
of the men I lead,
the men that lead me,
The men that saved me.
If I am never anything else I'll have been proud to be;
1st Battalion, 6th Marines.
We were Harder Than We Had to Be.

THE COMPANY YOU KEEP —————

I started out in Weapons,
full of Warriors through and through.
Specialized for specific jobs,
support is what we do.
Our biggest platoon is the 81's
heavy mortar men.
We call them the Shady Bums
they're degenerates to the end.
Then there are the CAAT platoons:
anti-tank missiles and heavy guns-
hard partying weirdos and massive goons
52s and 31s.
We also have the sniper teams,
they're pretty fuckin legit,
skull dragging long guns through the mud
to do clandestine shit

Then there's Alpha, or Apache
and I fuck with them boys too.
I catch em out on the catwalks and
stop to have some brews.
Them boys went to Spain and Italy
and partied 1/6 Hard
I've heard unbelievable stories about libo
at European festivals
and one about a stolen car.
Their 11s are pretty yoked up,
they can move some heavy weight.
They had the most POG First Sergeant in the Corps,
It's why they're so full of hate.

Then there's Bravo Blackfoot,
full of some of my best friends.
I've known that animal Savino
since my fucking contract began.
He's in a weapons platoon
full of gung ho and disgruntled brutes.
I used to love watching Jamie scream
while he was fucking up his boots.
There's Kaloudis and Kordic and Duran
and good ol' Jimmy Waitz
you can find them hitting weights,
sweating out the booze,

and working out the hate.
There's Pop Pop, Heckler,
Deveau, and Theriot
one of the best weapons platoons
you could ever get to know.

I first deployed with Charlie,
they call themselves Cold Steel.
I miss those motherfuckers,
they always kept it real.
You got Murder 3rd, Dunham's Boys,
they called him Daddy D.
Love the man or hate him,
he treats you like family.
I love my boys in Charlie Guns,
the best at gunnery,
and we all miss a man called Bloodlust...
Rest in Peace Sergeant Gee.
All day I could list the men I miss
that I'll have to go to hell to see,
NOT HEAVEN!
God can't let in that much sin
from all those savage 0311's.

I'm a civilian these days and I'm
alone now, nobody understands
the brotherhood and bonds we form
getting shit on by our command.
My unit was 1/6 HARD
and we rolled fucking deep.
You couldn't go wrong in that Battalion
No matter the Company you keep.

Our bodies will tell you stories.
Triceps tell you infantry, or just USMC,
either way, kin to me.
Vertically, tattooed 03.
Mostly elevens,
forty-ones with the spades,
and those like me,
31s.
Basilone's bastard sons,
Red Indian head,
because I was a 1/6 Hard one.
Cyclic rate of the needle and ink drum,
tattoo gun hums,
machine guns run.
We get tattoos like run away guns.
How much ink could we squeeze
out of tax refunds?
KA-Bars and stripes and stars,
they used to sleeve out when they were getting CARs.
Spider web elbows and American traditional,
get them grandfathered in so they're inadmissible.
"DIE MOTHERFUCKER DIE" around my thigh,
belt fed or dead, skulls staring back
from sunken eye sockets in their heads.
Love the sting, love the hurt, the burn,
covered in tattoos we had to earn,
hard lessons, the hard way, how we learn.
Pain retains the ink stains.
Some say unit and MOS tattoos
are boot moves like one ribbon dress blues.
Even if you didn't ink up,
don't think you're good as gold,
don't listen to all you're told.
Even with bare skin,
when you're no longer in
You'll see that EGA
was tattooed on your soul.

2.4-7 HURT LOCKER

I don't understand it, the panic,
after four years of chow halls and Domino's calls,
I forgot how to shop for groceries.
Something so simple makes me tense.
None of it makes sense.
Pushing the cart anxiously,
eyes avoiding others aggressively,
Unable to pinpoint what it is
that's stressing me.
Barely remember how to cook,
only know one recipe.
I don't know where anything is, nor do I have a list
of what I came for in the first place.
I feel my heart race.
Brain completely rewired to move through
OODA loop combat mindset
split decision making,
I stand there, my head shaking
I am full blown code black shut down,
overwhelmed by the plethora of possible purchases,
Paralyzed by the sheer and utter insignificance of it
all.
What to do with all this choice?
I would ask where the items are
if I could just find my voice…
From the bottom to the top shelf I look in confusion-
Although I could patrol all night in stealth
now I'm unsure of how to feed myself
or take care of my health,
wondering how to budget
when disability is my only income
and I have no wealth.
I feel like a lost child,
someone please help.
Is this what I've been reduced to?
A hungry veteran staring in anxiety
at a variety of frozen foods?

2.4-8 BURN IT DOWN

Flat range to ease the shooting pains
of life rearranged,
never the same,
empty home- ex and family and friends estranged.
Signed away those four years and everything
changed.
Gas it up to burn it down
round by round,
a stranger in my own hometown.
Transition to a forgotten life has me down.
Sight picture and breathing and trigger control
filling paper silhouettes with bullet holes.
Lonely and cold, carbon covered soul,
I didn't realize my choices would
take such tolls.
Controlled pairs,
hammers pair
and a clean headshot,
smile at the groups knowing
it would make a man stop and drop
after the round ripped through his top.
Shooting and moving from 50 in, at 25 the fun begins,
smooth and in control of speed reloads,
fresh mag, round chambered,
ready to explode.
Trained myself to master these skills and combat
mindset
while my life began to implode.
Silence and loneliness
overwhelms me,
tells me
to turn these guns on myself,
not as often since I put the liquor on the shelf,
and finally got help.
Used to do these drills with all my brothers.
When the gun goes dry I wish they were around,
I'm shooting just to hear the sound,
going cyclic calms me down,
round after round after round-
I gassed my life up just to burn it down.

2.4-9 HAUNTED ───────────────

There's a black leather bag on the shelf, gold zipper
busted by the words
written by my Recruit self-
Oh, the stories those old love letters tell,
Well, I was training for my own Hell, hypnotized and
brainwashed by that
Left-Right-Left Spell
I thought a war would be quite swell,
the only thing I loved more than her
Was that gun line smell,
and watching cannons vomit their artillery shells.

There's a check-in sheet there on the desk-
Drove 160 miles an hour chasing my own death,
officer could smell it on my breath,
Satan laughed at me in jail, to him it was a jest.
Regimental XO handled all the rest,
on restriction O.O.D. said I could've been the best.

There's two boxes with green and gold NAMs,
Heavy Guns Platoon called it the NAM Scam,
how this Marine got two, I still can't understand,
but in front of the Company I did stand,
humbled to shake the Fallujah Vet's hand.
Think I got it because I was the only one who still gave
a God Damn-
Cloth and a gold star I didn't deserve,
to tell the truth I find it quite absurd,
consolation prizes for a Terminal Lance,
Command finding new ways to polish up a turd.

There's a gold bordered flag blood red, covered in the
words that my brothers all said.
I worked for my heroes whose own brothers are dead-
Brings a tear to my eye and fills me with dread,
I see their faces at night
when I try to go to bed.

There's a handgun and a 12 inch KA-Bar,
both black as the night for dirty deeds in the dark.
When the loneliness gets heavy and hard-
can't pick which one to point at my cold dead heart.

2.4-10 WISH

I wish my brain would stop thinking
as much as my loved ones wished
I would stop drinking.
I wish I was a better swimmer, but my density
has got me sinking.

I wish I didn't see you anymore in my dreams.
I wish when I finally got some solitude,
my inner voice wasn't an unceasing scream.
I felt more at peace in a hole in the woods
eating MREs with my gun teams.

I wish my homecoming was a better reason to rejoice.
I wish my sacrifices didn't make people see me
as a victim of my choice.
I wish when I spoke they'd listen to my words,
not just hear my voice.

I wish my mind wasn't always racing.
Living back at home,
mother wonders why I'm always pacing.
I wish I could figure out what it was, exactly,
I spent all those years chasing.

I'm grateful for the brothers
I met in the Corps,
but I wish we weren't so hung up
On going to war.
There are no answers to your questions
on the other side of that door.
To this day nobody can tell me
what we were still over there for.

I wish he'd called someone before he died,
to get an idea of how much we'd all cry.
I forgive him because I suffer from the same kind of
pride.
I've had my own conversations with suicide.

I wish I could say I'm better than I've ever been,
but this is the first time I've ever been a veteran.
I regret nothing and would do it all over again.
I guess this is how it will be from now until the very
end:
Staring holes through the walls as Alice in Chains sings
Rotten Apple...
Wishing these wishes and missing my friends.

2.4-11 ECHOES

All my life I wanted more
Wanted more
Mom said be careful what you ask for
Ask for
Recruiter said it's only four
Only four
So I left home and joined the Corps
Joined the Corps
Yellow footprints on the floor
On the floor
They herded us through the doors
Through the doors
My life before now Nevermore
Nevermore
They sent me off to fight my war
Fight my war
Couldn't tell ya what I'm fighting for
Fighting for
Finally home still wanting more
Wanting more
Home doesn't feel like home anymore
Anymore
Drink until I hit the floor
Hit the floor
Can't remember life before the Corps
Before the Corps
No she doesn't talk to me anymore
Anymore
But I'm not the victim that's for sure
That's for sure
At times the villain more or less
More or less
A dirty secret I must confess
Must confess
I'd do it all again with no regrets
No regrets
To tell the truth about the Corps
About the Corps
I knew exactly what I was asking for
Asking for

2.4-12 DECORATED

You will not fully understand why
the attention to detail of the
placement of the
Ribbons,
Badges,
Medals,
Lengths,
Inseams,
Asymmetries,
and all those fucking goddamned IPs,
is so stressed at boot camp-
the geometry and symmetry,
the pomp and circumstance.
Attention to detail as if it were
being done for a dead man-
No you won't even begin to understand
until you're carefully pinning perfectly onto pressed
dress blues
your own earned ribbons
to bury a man who earned them with you.
Only when the familiar sound of TAPS
for once makes you cry,
when you flinch as the reporting rifles
crack hate at the sky,
when they fold the flag to present to his widow,
never again to fly-
You'll weep the day you understand why
your DI
was so stressed,
aggravated, and agitated
over how your uniform was
Decorated.

COCKTAILS

And now, finally, that my service is over
I can make an honest attempt to be sober.
This Christmas Eve at my Dad's
will be the driest one I've ever had.
Last time we all drank together
it was cold January weather,
I played my part, wore the blues
and eulogized our matriarch.
The water was Holy and blood was thicker,
Were you there when I tried to pummel my brother
after guzzling the liquor?
It's the key ingredient in my sick cocktail,
the vicious cycle set to fail.
Offset the alcohol with caffeine and nicotine,
chasing the dopamine.
I would rather die than take the SSRI,
I chase serotonin off of the adrenaline high-
Deny depression and give the impression
that everything is fine,
incapable of choosing water over wine,
Take the wheel and drive,
Foot to the floor, see if I survive-
Risk taking behavior is the flavor
of the bitter bourbon cocktail that kills so well.
Rapid rate cyclic shots
for suppression of the depression,
kill the inhibition and ignore the mission.
It's all violence and speed in my head
and when it goes quiet I'd rather be dead.
The connections are all broken and unreadable,
I am now quiet and anxious around other people.
It's all fight or flight, I only did wrong
when I wanted to do right, night after night.
Unexplained anger wells and swells and yells
and wants to fight and raise hell.
I am putting down the bottle
and easing off the throttle,
leaving the liquor on the shelf
and sitting quietly with myself.
Who am I after the Marines Corps?
Mind a dark room with no exit doors,
broken pieces of my life shattered all over the floor.
I don't want these cocktails anymore.

2.4-14 HANGOVER

It's been a long time since the last day
I wore cammies.
I will never have to run three miles for time again,
and how many pull ups I can do
no longer has any bearing on my worth as a person.
I'll never shoot a machine gun again.
I'm not on any roster to deploy.
My hair has grown out,
far longer than the standards,
and unfortunately
thinned from the stress.
Nobody says "Rah" or "Kill" anymore
because,
well,
that's insane.
I heard so many staff NCOs say
whether you do four or twenty
it doesn't really matter,
it's just how you do it.
My four year party,
my world tour
as part of the greatest warfighting branch in history,
the big green war machine,
left me with a lingering hangover
in the form of one question:

Was I a good Marine?

2.4-15 INSOMNIA —————————————

I never wanted it to end this way:
Disillusioned, like the ones who went before me.
The mission was to Make Marines, Win Battles, and return
as quality citizens…
And maybe I am a quality citizen now, if all that means
is
I follow the gun laws and don't drink and drive or get
in bar fights
Anymore…
I am an empty can that rattles loud, hollowed out.
I lost something in that Gun Club, or
maybe I truly gave it all away while I gave it my all.
Went in with youth, left old.
Went in fit, left with a limp.
Went in with a lover, left alone.
Went in as an idealist, left as a nihilist.
I gave away every last thing
to this thing that couldn't care about me.
Made it home alive
with no remnants of my ambition or drive.
My passion is out of action,
another burnt out cigarette,
given this title to wear: "Veteran"
Fits me no better than
"Marine" ever did,
it feels like I got out and ran away and hid.
Father asks "what's the matter?"
Thousand yard stare at a life shattered.
No idea what I'm doing here,
nothing left to give my Corps anymore,
wondering if this is what I feel like a failure for.
Insomnia in the bed I made,
I never wanted it to end this way.

2.4-16 BLACK BRACELETS, TOO ━━━

To my Junior Marines,
I am sorry for your loss-
My hearts breaks for you-
Now you wear black bracelets, too.

I didn't really know him,
he broke early, but surely,
I saw his potential, the same as I did
in all of you,
but when a Marine breaks early there's nothing we can
do-
I took the hate for him and
gave it to the rest of you-
It's the job that seniors have to do.

I know you loved him as your brother;
I was the motherfucker
coming up with the bullshit to put you all through.
You all become like little brothers to me
while he was medically separated
from the USMC.
I don't know what happened to him
while I was raising y'all up from Marine infancy.

I've lost one of my own to suicide.
I don't know why we can't stem the tide.
I wish they would all decide
it's better to just call a brother and confide.

This is part of growing up in the Marine Corps,
we're still losing brothers
with or without the war
and it's gonna hurt when someone asks you
what that bracelet is for,
when you put it on you'll realize
it's the heaviest thing you ever wore.

2.4-17 BUDDY, BUDDY, YOU'LL BE OKAY —

It's been over fifteen hundred days
since my Knowledge Hat taught me the words to say
to my brother Marines I find in a bad way:
"Buddy, Buddy, you'll be okay."

Whether he's barely grazed or missing limbs,
this is what you say to your close friends,
to calm him down and stay with him,
to get him back in the fight again.
I've found there are some types of trauma
that we can't see,
hidden hemorrhages in the psyche,
depression, anxiety, PTSD.
Ashamed to admit sometimes they even affect me.

You seemed in a dark place on your snapchat story
and I remembered all the times you'd been there for me.
You're right brother, this isn't something that I owe
you.
These phone calls are just what brothers should do.
So I just wanted to call on my drive home to say
"Buddy, Buddy, you'll be okay."

2.4-18 DUNNAGE

I wouldn't blame you if you felt anger
When I work up the nerve to light up your phone
once every 8 months or so.
No, I wouldn't blame you if it was all just
bitter frustration and blame left for me,
for as I've said you were my best friend,
I know I was yours too.
Yet the tragic trajectories of the tracers
of my wrong turns tumbled and burned
through the soft tissue of your heart,
the terminal ballistics of our coming apart.
We've done a few damage assessments together since
then,
between deployments.
In the silences when we reconnected,
you'd slip in small new interests and hobbies to tell me
of,
intimacies I no longer deserved.
But now that I don't have to pack up and go back to the
Marines,
I understand why you'd say
"Why bother?"
I suppose it would've been a better ending
if I'd died in combat,
just be dog tags
or a black bracelet
left to be loved and remembered by,
if I could be a spirit that lives on in your heart,
instead of a living ghost that haunts you.
I would understand if you answered my call to come back
by saying I've never really come back,
ever,
since the first day I left.
Only the words that I write left.

That damned Corps burned
away all of the gunpowder passion
that made me the man you loved,
and all that's left is the dunnage.

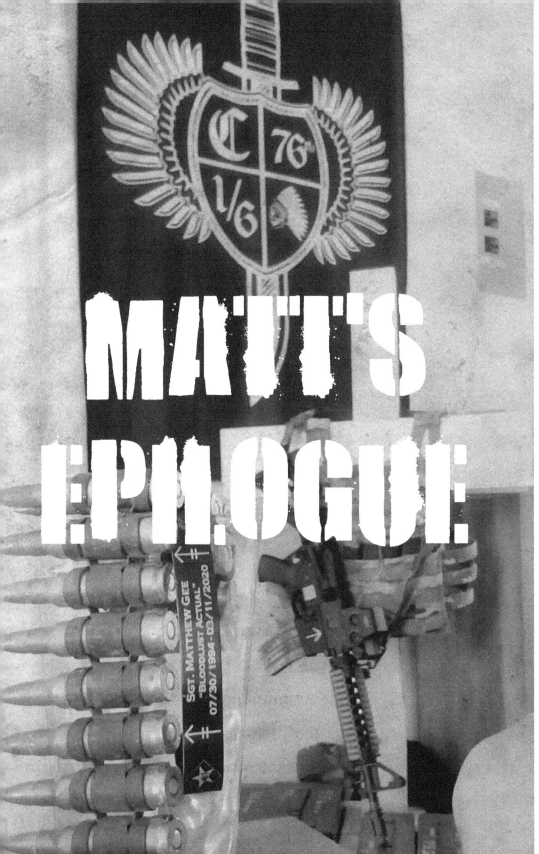

MATT'S
EPILOGUE

E.1. JAEGER

I'm not drinking a Jaeger for you
every fucking year.
Truth be told, Matt,
these days I barely even drink beer.
When I consume alcohol alone
missing everyone brings me to tears.
Beers bring on those kind of thoughts
we all fear.
Sad news no one wants to
but bitterly expects to hear
22 a day
8,030 a year.

No, Matt, I'm not gonna drown sorrows
in some liquor I don't even like.
Sinking in my misery
overflowing from the dike,
memories of you leading us
Charlie Guns on the hike.

I'll remember and honor you in better ways
by the actions I do and the words I say.
You stood by my side in my darkest days.
You believed in me at my lowest point,
when I had gone astray.
But now you're a weathered black bracelet
I look at every day.

It's a shame you're not around to see
the men all your boots will grow up to be.
We've got the watch,
it's all secure.
We'll carry on your legacy.

They say suicide is a selfish way to die,
I can't lie, I myself often wonder why,
here we are, Hard men reunited to cry.
I have howled at the moon and punched at the rain when
the liquor loosened my pain like a runaway train.
I've thrown your bracelet across the barracks room
floor
and cursed you for deciding
not to be here anymore, but I can't stay
mad at you because I've had the same thoughts before,
they still come to me even after the Corps.
If I did the same it wouldn't be the most selfish thing
I'd ever done,
it was pretty selfish of me to decide to live and die by
the gun,
a choice for my own desires that so darkly impacted my
loved ones.
A Constitution to defend and uphold, or so we're told,
called brave and bold,
enlisting for fool's gold in wars twenty years old
while enemies domestic our rights slowly stole.
That Selfless Selfish Oath betrothed us to our Corps
Honor, Courage, and Commitment
gave way to Hate, Greed, and Resentment.
Parents, Wives, children and girlfriends
take the Back Seat Row to the Big Fucking Show
We come and we go, the First to Fight and the Last to
Know.
Employment for deployment much to our enjoyment
Chasing violence to feed our egos, don't you know?
Adrenaline seeking HellHounds loading grenades into feed
throats.
Come home mixed up, fucked up, in love
with The Suck and only want to Re-Up for the next nut
causing divorces, no prenups and short sighted break
ups...
I couldn't wake up
from the spell of the infantry, trance it had on me,
I guess the same thing happened to Gee
He lived and died for this Cut Throat Corps and
his new unit didn't love him back
like the family he had before,
this fickle whore always asking for another four,

but zero defects, if not perfect, she'll show you the
door.
Wish I could've stopped him from pulling the trigger
just like he wished he'd stopped me from guzzling the
liquor
and putting pedal to the floor,
decisions haunting others forevermore.
As far as Marines and men go he was one of the great
ones,
I lived far more selfishly than he died,
that's why onto my blues I cried
and flinched as the hateful report of the guns
screamed our sorrow at the sky.
I ask God How but I actually know Why,
Giants come home and commit suicide.

I fucking followed you.
You were a fucking gunfighter,
a professional.
Brother, this is my
betrayed confessional.
You fucking lived for
this Corps,
gave them four more.
Was living for War not enough for you?
Why did you think you had to
die for it too?
Did you think about us before you dropped pack,
and how much we all looked up to you?
Two pumps to the sandbox, no CAR,
I heard 2/7 was telling you to kick rocks?
What did you want?
Finally, one kill, with one shot?
You gave the Corps your left arm
to glorify our violent history-
Frozen Chosin machine gun pride,
Vietnam Pig on belt fed bicep resides,
Belleau Woodsman forearm
bayoneting the Hun in the chest,
0331 said the rest.
Tricep Cold Steel Family crest…
You broke your families' heart
and your little brothers are picking up
shattered pieces of what's left.
Why
Couldn't you call anyone before
you decided you rate to die?
Didn't you know how much
your brothers would cry?
You left me with questions
the answers to which I'll never know.
You were my leader,
but you went to a place I won't go.
Suicide is an example
I fight my own battles not to follow.
Losing a senior is a sorrow
I swear I won't ever
make your grand boots know.

Bro,
I'm fucking sorry
that you had to go.
We loved you,
but I guess you didn't know.

E.4. IT TAKES SOMETHING TO FEEL ALIVE ———

Matt, you had "It Takes Something to Feel Alive"
tattooed on your ribs.
It did, in fact, take a lot to feel alive, Matt.
It took poetry, so much fucking poetry.
It took crying.
Just crying, by myself, alone with my words.
It took sharing them
with brothers
in the barracks
in moments of vulnerability.
It took the courage to start an Instagram page
to put it out in the community.
It took a lot of conversations
with veterans and active duty alike,
that I didn't even know,
but who needed to talk.
It took swallowing my pride and living at my Mom's
as a thirty year old man
after leaving the Marines.
It took saying yes to opportunities
and no to suicidal thoughts.
It took so many VA appointments
after being trained to not advocate for myself.
It took paying a grand out of pocket a month
for trauma informed therapy
because the VA couldn't accommodate my work schedule.
It took 60-80 hours a week
at the refinery swinging sledge hammers
and pulling chains in the heat.
It took walking away from six figures.
It took going to Montana.
It took volunteering for the rest of the month.
It took moving to New Orleans
when I didn't know anybody there anymore.
It took finally letting go of her.
It took everything Matt, and
I give what's asked and then some.
It takes risks, and healing yourself,
learning to believe in yourself,
and knowing when to ask for help.

It takes love, and to this day I love you brother.
I put your name all over this book,
sometimes in anger,
sometimes in sadness,
but here I just want the record to show
that you were an incredible man,
brother,
Marine,
and bona fide Rock Eater.

GRUNT TO ENGLISH TRANSLATIONS—

03- the field designation for "infantry"

1/6- 1st Battalion 6th Marine Infantry Regiment, the hardest fucking grunt unit on the East Coast, possibly the Marine Corps, we'll fight you

11- short for 0311, a Marine Rifleman, the main effort and tip of the spear of the Marine Corps

2nd award- "2nd award" is a term rewarded after qualifying expert a second time in a row on rifle or pistol qualification, used sarcastically after someone is demoted to a rank already had, can also apply to 3rd award, etc

240- M240B, the medium machine gun of the U.S. military, feels really badass to carry on foot

31- short for 0331, the military occupational specialty for machine gunner, the baddest motherfuckers on planet Earth, do not fuck with them, they'll hurt you, all of them, at the same time, really bad, and laugh about it while doing it

50- M2/.50 cal/"Ma Deuce," the heavy machine gun of the U.S. military, weighs 86 pounds total and fires 450-600 rounds per minute, not fun to carry on foot

72- three day weekend

81s- 81 mm mortar platoon, members of these platoons are a hazard to your health, complete degenerates, completely impervious to disciplinary action, and really fucking good at dropping mortars on people far away while playing cards in a hole they dug in the ground

ACOG- ("ay-cog") Advanced Combat Optical Gunsight, 4x magnified optic used on M4 rifles

Attention- standing with arms locked to side and feet together, seriously, don't lock your knees or you'll pass out in formation, you stupid boot, it'll be super fucking embarrassing because none of your friends are allowed to break the position of attention to catch you or carry your stupid ass away, and they'll probably lose their bearing and laugh at you for being a stupid boot

Battalion- three "line" companies of rifleman and weapons specialized Marines and one weapons company of heavy weapons Marines along with a headquarters & support company

BC- battalion commander

BDC- bullet drop compensator, used to account for the drop of a bullet when aiming at longer distances

Black bracelet- black memorial bracelets worn by service members, originally for fellow service members killed in action (KIA) and increasingly more and more for those lost to suicide (if you have a problem with these being worn for suicides, seriously get the fuck over yourself)

Boot- new Marine/junior Marine (also, everyone is a boot to somebody)

Boot drop- when a group of Marines graduate and ITB and are sent to an infantry battalion, this is the worst time in a Marine's life by far

Bricks- barracks

CAAT- pronounced "cat" combined anti-armor team, a vehicle-mounted platoon of heavy machine gunners and anti-tank missile-men, we're better than you

CAR- Combat Action Ribbon, awarded for participating in combat, often legitimately, sometimes bogusly, not worth being insecure about

Chow- food, eating a meal

CIF- combat issue facility, probably, I didn't actually look up what this stood for, but it's where you're issued your gear, and in true government fashion, they make you clean it a million fucking times before they'll accept it back

CO- commanding officer, usually used to refer to a company commander

Company- three rifle platoons and one weapons platoon

Condition one- round in the chamber, weapon ready to fire

Corpsman- Navy Corpsman, medical personnel within the Navy, Corpsmen who go "Green Side" become platoon medics or "Docs" for Marines

Cowboy coffee- coffee made in a jet boil

CP- command post, in garrison this is the location of the company and battalion offices

Crucible- 54-hour training evolution in the field, culminating event of Marine boot camp, not actually that hard, suck it the fuck up

Cyclic- the rate of fire of a machine gun when one doesn't shoot in bursts, shooting non-stop until the source of ammunition runs out

DI- Drill Instructor, AKA basically your own personal Satan

Dunnage- the leftover brass, and for machine guns, links after shooting at the range, all dunnage is to be police called to be turned in somewhere

Duty- one NCO and junior Marine on duty for 24 hour periods that report to the OOD and help them make sure that Marines don't do bad shit off of work

EGA- the Eagle, Globe, and Anchor, the insignia of the United States Marine Corps, just looking at it makes Marines fill with bloodlust and become fully erect

Field Day- usually Thursday, when Marines are expected to clean their bombed-out shithole barracks to high standards for inspection by their company First Sergeant the following morning, used by seniors to fuck with juniors by imposing unrealistic standards, completely necessary to build and maintain good order and discipline but also a massive pain in the ass

Field op- a training exercise in the field

The Fleet- Fleet Marine Forces, the fighting and deploying units of the Marine Corps and all units that support them directly, the real Marine Corps

FOB- forward operating base

Frag- grenade

FROG- Fire Retardant Operational Gear, uniforms worn on deployment, way cooler than regular cammies

GWOT- Global War on Terror, an umbrella term for all combat operations carried out "against terrorism" after 9/11

HP- Hadnot Point barracks, occupied mainly by infantry on Camp Lejeune, jokingly called the "Hadnot Projects" because of the state of damage and disarray they are in from decades of housing young Marines with little to no repairs

IED- improvised explosive device, bombs made of homemade products and hidden along routes to launch complex ambushes on U.S. service members, a key weapon of the insurgents of the GWOT in every country it occurred in

IPAC- I don't know what this stands for, but this is where all the Admin Marines work, and every time I ever went there, I was like, "what the fuck kind of bizarro Marine Corps is this? They all literally only work in an office. What the fuck"

Internal- based on Cooper's Color Code of Awareness, with white being totally unaware of anything going on and black being so totally and utterly overwhelmed by one's circumstances that they "go internal" and can't react. In field training environments, it is often said that Marines are "going internal" when the situation is so fucked through rain, unbearable cold, or other very unpleasant conditions that they just sort of stop giving a fuck

IT- extra training, often held on the quarterdeck of the squad bay, often as correction for any and all mistakes made by a recruit or group of recruits, gets you so in shape that by the end of boot camp, you're like, "fuck it I'll go get IT'd with that kid that still can't figure out how to tie a fucking shoe, holy fucking shit I can't believe he's gonna graduate"

ITB- Infantry Training Battalion, two-month training block for Marines after boot camp where they learn the military occupational specialty of infantry and then become riflemen, machine gunners, mortarmen, assaultmen, or anti-tank gunners; not a good time

ITX- Integrated Training Exercise, the final training event of most work-ups held in the deserts of California, usually lasting one to two months, where an infantry unit integrates with air support, heavy artillery, and tanks on large scale ranges

Jody- the military term for dudes who fuck wives and girlfriends of military service members while said service members are deployed

Kill Hat- DI responsible for the discipline of recruits (yes, Marines name everything with most violent title possible)

M9- service pistol

MCMAP- Marine Corps Martial Arts Program, not as badass as it sounds, trust me

Mk19- pronounced Mark 19, 77 lb grenade machine gun, even less fun to carry, but dudes will basically suck you off if you don't pass it off during a hike

NCO- non commissioned officers, Corporals, and Sergeants that hold senior leadership roles within a platoon

NJP- non-judicial punishment, at minimum 14 days of restriction (house arrest) to a barracks room, at the most loss of rank by one rank and 60 days of restriction and extra duties, used as punishment for a wide variety of disciplinary issues

OOD- Officer of the Day, a Staff NCO and officer in charge of making sure the Marines don't cannibalize each other and burn the barracks to the ground during non-working hours and weekends

OSO- Officer Selection Office, where kids in college go to not use their college degree for four years if they can run really fast and didn't get any DUIs

Parade Rest- standing with hands behind back and legs shoulder with apart, don't lock your knees out in this position because it makes some people, possibly you, pass out

PFT- physical fitness test, conducted annually, a combination of pull-ups (max score 23), crunches (max score 115) and a 3-mile run (max score 18 minutes), total score factors heavily into promotion rates, because, ya know, leadership is basically just how fast you can run

Police call- cleaning up trash, often done as a group shoulder to shoulder walking across an area, used to pick up the brass on a range or garbage in the garrison barracks area, definitely not used at all by senior Marines to keep junior Marines busy until they get off work or to pick up beer cans and bottles and cigarette butts after a barracks party

POG- persons other than grunts, most are cool, some have little dick complex, and if they have any kind of rank whatsoever, they shit on junior enlisted grunts for minor uniform infractions in public, and it's all very juvenile

PT- physical training

PVS14- night vision monocle used for nighttime operations and training

PX- post exchange, like a big ass mall on base

Rack- bed, except less comfortable

RBE- Remain Behind Element, Marines not deployed with a unit due to injury, lack of time on contract, or serious legal trouble, my company integrated and took command of the Battalion RBE because we deployed to Syria before our battalion did their main deployment and did not join them

Recruit- trainee in boot camp, lower than a worm, basically undeserving of any human rights because they literally signed a contract agreeing to it

Reveille- a signal sounded to wake people in the armed forces, in the field, it's just whatever boot had the last fire watch (staying awake and standing guard in shifts) and has to scream "REVEILLE, REVEILLE, REVEILLE"

RO- radio operator, very underrated and under appreciated role in the infantry platoon

ROE- Rules of Engagement, conditions determined by the U.S. government that determines when service members can or can not engage an enemy

SAW- Squad Automatic Weapon, a belt-fed machine gun that shoots rifle caliber rounds

Semper Fi- Semper Fidelis, or Always Faithful, the motto of the Marine Corps

SGLI- Service-members Group Life Insurance

STA- Surveillance and Target Acquisition, also known as Scout Snipers, they're as badass as you think they are, sick fucks, they'll low crawl through a mile of shit to shoot a guy they've never met through the face once

TEEP- training effectiveness and evaluation plan

Teufel Hunden- German for "Devil Dog" or "hellhound," nickname given to the Marines during the battle of Belleau Wood in WWI, probably misspelled every time it was ever written by a Marine, whatever, they should've not let so many Marines stab them in the chest if they wanted us to learn German

UA- unauthorized absence, not that big of a deal unless you're UA for 30 (or was it 29?) days, at which point you're AWOL, or Absent Without Leave, and then the Government comes looking for you, which is preferable for some to actually being in the Marine Corps

WAKEF- stop in the local language in Syria; I yelled this at people like a total boot while cordoning off IEDs, and I probably didn't even say it right

Weapons Company- CAAT, 81s, and STA platoons

Work-up- 12-18 month training period prior to deployment, can be shortened for short-notice deployments

XO- executive officer

COLLECTIVE

DEAD RECKONING COLLECTIVE is a veteran owned and operated publishing company. Our mission encourages literacy as a component of a positive lifestyle. Although DRC only publishes the written work of military veterans, the intention of closing the divide between civilians and veterans is held in the highest regard. By sharing these stories it is our hope that we can help to clarify how veterans should be viewed by the public and how veterans should view themselves.

Visit us at:

deadreckoningco.com

 @deadreckoningcollective

 @deadreckoningco

 @DRCpublishing

Follow MASON RODRIGUE

@deadgunnerpoetry

MASON RODRIGUE was born between a bayou and a sugar cane field in Louisiana to an alligator and a mafia hitman. He attended LSU to extend his football career farther than it should have gone in the first place and eventually settled for playing rugby. He enlisted in the Marine Corps as a machine gunner to live out his dream of professionally reenacting scenes from Rambo and was sentenced to Camp Lejeune, North Carolina. After deploying to Syria, a series of self-destructive life choices (even for a Marine) left him broke, depressed, and identifying as "a writer." He is a proud recipient of a Regimental NJP and finally earned the rank of Corporal in the IRR. He now lives in New Orleans, where he drinks at the VFW, stockpiles ammo, and works on building a civilian legal Squad Automatic Weapon.

CPSIA information can be obtained
at www.ICGtesting.com
Printed in the USA
JSHW021917140623
43249JS00001B/69